S0-BLP-554

# LITERARY CRITICISM AND CULTURAL THEORY

*Edited by*

## William E. Cain
Professor of English
Wellesley College

A ROUTLEDGE SERIES

# LITERARY CRITICISM AND CULTURAL THEORY

WILLIAM E. CAIN, *General Editor*

# COSMOPOLITAN FICTIONS
## Ethics, Politics, and Global Change in the Works of
## Kazuo Ishiguro, Michael Ondaatje,
## Jamaica Kincaid, and J. M. Coetzee

Katherine Stanton

Routledge
New York & London

Published in 2006 by
Routledge
Taylor & Francis Group
270 Madison Avenue
New York, NY 10016

Published in Great Britain by
Routledge
Taylor & Francis Group
2 Park Square
Milton Park, Abingdon
Oxon OX14 4RN

© 2006 by Taylor & Francis Group, LLC
Routledge is an imprint of Taylor & Francis Group

Printed in the United States of America on acid-free paper
10 9 8 7 6 5 4 3 2 1

International Standard Book Number-10: 0-415-97542-5 (Hardcover)
International Standard Book Number-13: 978-0-415-97542-1 (Hardcover)

---

**Library of Congress Cataloging-in-Publication Data**

---

Catalog record is available from the Library of Congress

---

Visit the Taylor & Francis Web site at
http://www.taylorandfrancis.com

Taylor & Francis Group
is the Academic Division of T&F Informa plc.

and the Routledge Web site at
http://www.routledge-ny.com

# Contents

# Acknowledgments

I am deeply grateful to Bruce Robbins, Derek Attridge, and Marianne DeKoven, perceptive and exacting readers who have sharpened my thinking—and shown me what's worth thinking about. I thank Marianne especially for always wanting to hear what I have to say. I also thank Bonnie Honig, whose careful reading of this study as a dissertation energized and informed this revision. Fellowships from the Rutgers Department of Literatures in English and Graduate School were important to the dissertation's completion; the encouragement of my colleagues Linda Hodges and Pamela Barnett at Princeton University's McGraw Center for Teaching and Learning was essential to its revision.

My editor at Routledge, Max Novick, was a beacon of good sense and good humor throughout the revision process. I owe a special thanks to Kendra McKnight, who brought her keen editorial eye to the pages that follow.

My parents, Pam Stanton and John Sawyer, have been an unwavering source of encouragement and support during the research, the writing, and the revising of this study. It is to them that it is dedicated. I owe much of the richness of my life in this period to my friendships with Tanya Agathocleous, Patricia Armstrong, Kim Bernhardt, Laurel Blatchford, Lisa Lynch, Anne Mansfield, Kendra McKnight, Nicole Merola, Kate Moran, and Cornelia Reiner.

Above all, I thank my husband John Scanlon, whose intellectual acuity and emotional generosity sustain and enliven me.

Introduction

# Contemporary Cosmopolitan Fictions

Responding to—indeed, participating in—what Giles Gunn terms the "loosening" of national paradigms for literary study (2001, p. 16), this study takes up the challenge that he poses. As Gunn sees it, the stretching of the field of literary study—for which a title like PMLA's "Globalizing Literary Study" serves as a shorthand—has reorganized the bounds of literary study "around sociopolitical histories of dominance, oppression, and opposition" (p. 16). Our challenge as critics, he argues, is to analyze not only how the cultural materials we study have been produced by globalizing trends, of which these contested histories are one part, but also how they have subjected those trends to scrutiny. This is the challenge that my study undertakes. Kazuo Ishiguro's *The Unconsoled,* Michael Ondaatje's *Anil's Ghost,* Jamaica Kincaid's *My Brother,* and J. M. Coetzee's *Age of Iron* and *Disgrace* take as their subjects and their objects of scrutiny the unification of Europe, the human rights movement, the AIDS epidemic, and the end of apartheid and the South African state's shift to neoliberalism. Like their authors—a Japanese-born "Englishman," a Canadian born in Sri Lanka, or, as Ondaatje calls it, Ceylon, an Antiguan-born US resident, and an English-speaking white South African—they possess international viewpoints. These works historicize the movements and networks of the transnational or the global, keeping their sights on the multiple histories of colonialism and imperialism that Gunn identifies. They recognize the various features of the newly pluralized and particularized cosmopolitanism, including the chosen or unchosen reasons for travel: professional demands, educational scholarships, familial desperation, and sexual trafficking. Featuring variously empowered protagonists—an internationally renowned pianist, a local daughter turned foreign celebrity, a newly privileged economic migrant, a "late" colonialist—these works contend with what Bruce Robbins describes as "the terrible inequalities of power and wealth that structure the world of nations" (1999, p. 5) and recognize that ethical responsibility and political action operate within, even as they stand or work against, such inequalities[1]; indeed, these fictions suggest that these inequalities make ethics and politics *more* pressing.

I have chosen to designate these works cosmopolitan fictions, signaling their interest in states of feeling, modes of belonging, and practices of citizenship in an increasingly pluralized cosmos[2]. Recent scholarship has revitalized and redefined the concept of cosmopolitanism, understanding it less as "an ideal of detachment" than as "a reality of (re)attachment, multiple attachment, or attachment at a distance" (Robbins, 1998, p. 3), while also making clear that it is neither an exclusively Western nor a necessarily privileged phenomenon. Rather than world citizenship, cosmopolitanism now indicates a multiplicity or diversity of belongings—some carefully cultivated, others reluctantly assumed. Meant as an interpretive lens as well as a descriptive term, "cosmopolitan fiction" can help us glean new insights into literary and cultural works, including contemporary works in English, the field I know best, that thematize migration, exile, and the diasporic condition. Viewed as a work of cosmopolitan fiction, Sara Suleri's *Meatless Days*, for instance, insisting that "there are no women in the third world" (1987, p. 20), raises the difficult question of feminist solidarity across borders. As they themselves grapple to varying degrees with the themes of migration, exile, and diaspora, the works in this study grapple with the sudden expansions and sharp retractions of community in the late-twentieth century that both vex and excite ethical and political allegiance.

To designate a literary genre as *cosmopolitan,* and to organize a study in this way, is not to claim that the nation is no longer a viable category of literary analysis (or lived experience). But it is to support the injunction that Paul Jay has convincingly made, that we make the nation the contested subject rather than the confirmed fact of our scholarly and pedagogical framework; in his analysis, literature departments should focus on understanding "the functional [rather than normative[3]] relation between literature [and not just contemporary literature] and the nation-state, how literary writing has been theorized and politicized in efforts to define and empower nation-states . . ." (2001, p. 42). The hesitation of Ishiguro and Coetzee to be read within national canons—Ishiguro considers himself a European rather than a British novelist (Ishiguro & Kenzaburo, 1991, p. 115)[4]; Coetzee rejects the term "South African" novelist—lends itself to this argument. Of course, as I point out, being South African is a way of being international, of gaining a certain prestige and marketability. Heeding Gayatri Chakravorty Spivak's imperative, I seek to "world" Coetzee's novels, to recognize and draw out, as his work does, the global histories that constitute South Africa. These histories may be given voice to in the "indigenous or native narrative" that is, in Homi Bhabha's words, "*internal to*" national identity (1994, p. 6, emphasis in the original), a narrative we might hear a whisper of in the voices of the "exotic" prostitutes whom the protagonist of *Disgrace* hires. Following the model of colonial and postcolonial studies, this kind of worlding—a process with contestory possibilities, as Bhabha's words here and elsewhere suggest[5]—is what a refocused program for literary study could do and what this study aims to do.

Testing the demands of justice against the shifting borders of the nation, the fictions I have gathered here recognize that ethical and political agency overhangs those borders. My readings demonstrate that they expand our capacities for ethical and political action into a global or cosmopolitical field. But they do more than that. Confronting the pervasiveness of ethical claims, the disjointing of the global field of action, and the impediments to social redistribution, these works, I argue, insist on a necessary negotiation between the ethical and the political. We may understand this as a negotiation between my responsibility to and for the other—a particular response owed to a particular other—and my responsibility to and for the other others—that same response owed to all the other others. Along with this negotiation between a singular and a universal responsibility, we may also understand the negotiation between the ethical and the political as one between meeting an obligation to and for the other(s) and making judgments about which of those obligations to meet, taking necessarily complex (and often unsatisfying) stances[6], participating in the public life of the nation, or acting collectively (within and perhaps across state borders) for systematic change and reform. We will see this negotiation play out within and across individual chapters, as I detail below. Together, these works complicate the common critical suspicion that "the turn to ethics is the turn away from politics . . ."[7] (Garber, Hanssen & Walkowitz, 2000, p. ix). Lawrence Buell identifies as "the touchiest single issue for both exemplars and critics of the ethical turn . . . whether it boils down, whatever the nominal agenda, to a privatization of human relations that makes the social and political secondary" (1999, p. 14). I remind us that ethics does not take place in a void or out of context—as Coetzee's fiction makes clear, our obligation or debt to the racial other *is* historical. Still, I acknowledge that "the starting point of obligation" may seem "suspiciously privatistic to many social and cultural constructionists, not to mention neo-Marxist materialists . . . ," and take seriously Buell's conclusion that ethical theorists "remain under pressure to demonstrate how exactly obligation might be understood as potent not only 'culturally' but also historically and politically" (p. 15). In her treatment of the AIDS epidemic, Kincaid's *My Brother*, I argue, in one response to this conclusion, suggests that a commitment to the singular and the contingent—to the specific demands and possibilities of the person or the situation—may, in fact, *sharpen* a political program, insisting on the testing and reaffirmation, not necessarily the rejection, of assumptions, predictions, generalizations, and laws.

To be clear, these works do not find ethics, the responsibility I have to and for the other(s) a *solution* or an *alternative* to politics: rather, they probe the interdependence of the ethical and the political. This interdependence is precisely where Simon Critchley and Richard Kearney locate deconstructive thinking's political force. Writing on the contradiction within the cosmopolitan tradition—and specifically, within Kantian thought—between the law of unconditional hospitality and the conditional limits on the rights of residence, Jacques Derrida makes evident that without the second imperative, the conditional limits, the first "would be in danger of remaining a pious and irresponsible desire, without form and without potency, and even of being perverted at any moment" (2001, p. 23). In their preface to *Cosmopolitanism and Forgiveness,* Critchley and Kearney put it this way: "[A]ll of the political difficulty of immigration consists in negotiating between these two imperatives" (2001, p. x). Derrida describes doing justice— actively respecting both sides of the tension—as experimental and inventive as well as ongoing and immediate; discussing the idea of the refuge city where the foreigner could seek sanctuary, he queries, could "the right to asylum be redefined and developed without repatriation and without naturalization? Could the City, equipped with new rights and greater sovereignty, open up new horizons of possibility previously undreamt of by international state law?" (2001, pp. 7–8). Imagining the city as a place to remake, to transform and improve, immigration law, he argues that the coupling in Kantian and Enlightenment thinking of the limits on hospitality with state sovereignty "is what remains for us debatable" (2001, p. 22); holding open or calling into question this coupling, he is spurred by both the rich history of hospitality within the Western tradition and the terrible failures of the state to protect the rights of asylum.

These fictions uncouple other conceptions, like citizenship, from nationality, and yet continue to attest to the persistence of the nation as, among other things, a structure of feeling. Their cosmopolitical thinking is not post-national, in other words. Recognizing that borders are "vacillating," in Étienne Balibar's words, they do not claim they have disappeared. He reminds us that national borders "are becoming the object of protest and contestation as well of an unremitting reinforcement, notably of their function of security" (1998, p. 220). This vacillation means "that borders have stopped

marking the limits where politics ends because the community ends"
(p. 220); indeed, these fictions recognize, with Balibar, how complicated our
notions of community, and their stopping and starting points, are. I take as
my starting point for the investigation into the ethics and politics of complex
belonging Ishiguro's *The Unconsoled,* in which I read the emotional hesitation
and withholding characteristic of his characters as indicative of the moment
when the closeness and legitimacy of claims on our attention and energy are
newly in question. Arguing that *The Unconsoled* is legible as a European
Union novel, my first chapter follows Ryder, the novel's protagonist, as he
arrives in a European city vaguely familiar to him and confronts a series of
demands on his attention—not least from a woman who appears to be his
wife. That his over-commitment prevents him from recognizing his home,
and from being fully present to his family, seems the grim conclusion that we
are to reach. Against the dominant trend of Ishiguro criticism, though, I take
Ryder's insignificant duties (to attend a dinner party, to support a local cause,
to listen to a struggling musician rehearse, and so on) as the source of the significant ethical point the novel is making. Representing as an everyday problem the tension between a singular and a universal responsibility, the novel
invites us to treat the problem of multiple demands *as* a problem to be struggled over: where, and on what terms, do we respond? Raising the question of
accountability for the transnational actor that Ondaatje's novel picks up, this
invitation has more generalizing powers if we heed Bruce Robbins's call to
master the sorts of allegiance and action that go with our complicated
belonging, a mastery that, I contend, the novel both respects and puts into
question. I pursue Ishiguro's ethical internationalism in an afterword on his
fifth novel, *When We Were Orphans,* revaluing the protagonist's "mistaken"
recognition of an enemy soldier as his long-lost friend.

 Ondaatje's *Anil's Ghost* puts pressure on *The Unconsoled*'s resistance to
mastery, reminding us that even if we resist *final* visions of justice, we must
constantly make judgments about what is just. The work finds a different
truth from Ondaatje's earlier memoir about Sri Lanka, which reconstructs a
family history and a place in it; opening with her arrival to Colombo on a
human rights investigation, the novel foregrounds Anil Tissera's realization
that she does not have any attachments to the place of her birth. And this
does not change—or rather, does not change in the way that her investigative
partner, Sarath Diyasena, wants it to. As the title of the novel signals, Anil is
haunted by the ghosts of the disappeared, one of whom she and Sarath track
through the killing fields of Sri Lanka. In the novel's sensitivity to the messiness of their human rights investigation, I notice its attention to the secular,
while acknowledging John McClure's argument for the religious practices of

retreat that make such work possible. I trace its development of what Bhabha might call a secular community—a different example of these works' worldly commitments—open to difference, disagreement, and risk. Without agreeing to Sarath's request that she stay after the investigation, Anil becomes citizenized through her participation in such a community. Imagining the possibility of citizenship uncoupled from state sovereignty, the novel sets this cosmopolitan practice against the unmitigated return that Sarath desires her to make *and* the version of Western visitorship that he critiques. The novel, undoing the opposition between foreign authority and citizen, also scrutinizes the limits of legal prosecution on a national level; the novel's premature closure—its elision of the process of arrest and trial for the perpetrators of human rights crimes—testifies to the absence of a court in which such a trial could happen.

Kincaid's *My Brother*, which documents Kincaid's conflicted relation to her brother Devon Drew and his death from AIDS-related illnesses, nuances the argument for cosmopolitan citizenship that Ondaatje makes, finding that global action takes place on an uneven field. I argue that the memoir both returns to and elaborates on the familiar narrative of Kincaid's "ruthlessness" towards her family; writing as a newly privileged member of the prosperous part of the world, she identifies ethical passivity with capitalist privilege. On the level of the text, Kincaid struggles to maintain an ethical stance towards Devon; extending Sarah Brophy's reading of her "tender rejection" of him, I pay attention to her unsympathetic portrait of him, her preservation of his vernacular, and her inability to find metaphors to describe his painful deterioration and death. This insistence on singularity has powerful implications for Kincaid's recognition that the epidemic requires not only an ethics but also a politics—a politics that, faced with the "scattered hegemonies" (Grewal & Kaplan, 1994) that result in the unavailability of antiretrovirals in the Caribbean, must exceed both state boundaries *and* the single issue. Kincaid implicates her readers as well as herself in the largely unrelieved suffering she observes; in a final section, I argue that the memoir itself figures as an act of what Bhabha calls vernacularization, bringing the global into the space of the metropolitan.

*Age of Iron* and *Disgrace*, which span the dismantling of apartheid and the inception of a new nation, participate as literature in a discussion about restitution as a mechanism of the economic justice so absent in Kincaid's memoir. Taking up the references to payment and ownership in *Age of Iron*, the fourth chapter finds in that novel an acknowledgment of the impossibility of fully meeting one's debt to the racial other: that is, the impossibility of full remission, or what Diane Elam calls "final redemption," for the crimes of apartheid. *Disgrace* offers a critique of restitution as an exchange of goods rather than a reform of structural inequalities, reform that both local and international capital have reason to resist. The novel queries gender's relationship to a just society; the brutal rape of Lucy Lurie is interpreted by her, and by certain of *Disgrace*'s critics, as a means of debt repayment. But the novel figures Lucy's embrace of her subjection as no choice at all. Its representation of another economy of exchange, the global traffic in women, sharpens its critical edge. *Disgrace* insists with Spivak that we think not only about how the world has abandoned Africa but also about what it finds there; South Africa, for instance, has become a destination for sex tourism. In this insistence that we consider what the world *finds* in South Africa, which echoes and deepens *My Brother*'s impulses, we can recognize Coetzee's refusal to write himself out of its post-apartheid future.

Spivak, Elam, and Cornell, whose insights I will turn to throughout this study, make clear that with the acknowledgement of the not-yet of justice comes the imperative of participation. Their thinking, and the urgency of their thinking, is informed not only by deconstructive theory but also by feminism; as feminist thinkers, they are cautious of final visions of justice and yet alert to multiple injustices. It is worth making clearer the tone or tones in which these works make this same feminist acknowledgement. *The Unconsoled*'s suggestion that there are always further demands to consider and negotiations or arbitrations to make isn't evasive or cynical; it doesn't mean that there *won't* be solutions to the problems of multiple or competing claims, solutions that may satisfy more than one of them—crucially important, and difficult, in the realm of conflicting loyalties and allegiances[8]. Likewise, the recognition that justice is beyond final definition or calculation in Coetzee's fictions—as Mrs. Curren in *Age of Iron* wonders, who could ever count the acts of labor performed under racial capitalism?—does not command inactivity or non-response. Rather, that novel's premise, as a letter to be sent on after death, extends the same invitation to ongoing engagement—in this case, towards reassessing the racialized distribution of benefits—that Ishiguro does. With the "power to break up the given, to admit and elaborate the possible" (1999, p. 16), as Andrew Gibson describes it, these works produce "what, with Adorno in mind, Cornell calls the 'redemptive perspectives' that 'displace and estrange the world,' so that 'we are made aware that we are in exile'" (p. 16). It is for their culturally elaborative powers that I choose "work" or "fiction" rather than "text" to refer to these cosmopolitan fictions[9]. While I am, in fact, concerned to read these works into history, to demonstrate their representational or referential qualities, I also attend to how they redefine and transfigure that history.

There is another way that these texts understand the not-yet or unfinished quality of justice: Kincaid's text recognizes that there is always more
that she could do for Devon. But this sobering recognition also stands
against the passivity that *My Brother* specifically identifies capitalism as pro-
moting. It is capitalism in its national and global forms, *rather than the
demands of justice themselves,* that both Kincaid's and Coetzee's works identify
as a source of ethical ennui and paralysis[10]. As these texts suggest—in Kincaid's insistence on framing the AIDS epidemic in terms of unequal standards of living, or in Coetzee's notice of the vast discrepancies between life
expectancies of white Americans and of black South Africans—capitalist
interests are also Northern interests; both pointedly and gently, they register
the link between them, making even more pressing Coetzee's critical attention to South Africa's entrance into the global economy. It is hardly coinci-
dental that Kincaid takes the state—that is, the United States, which, until a
few years ago, maintained a policy of intimidation against countries that
made or bought generic antiretrovirals through compulsory licensing[11]—as
her alibi for the limits of her willingness to help her estranged brother. I trace
a contestory response to another form of indifference that the current Bush
administration holds towards those outside its borders through Ondaatje's
novel, which, establishing a global framework for legality, poses a challenge
to its unwillingness to be subject to internationally binding treaties.

These works illuminate different aspects of ethics and politics in a
global world—the necessity of judging domestic matters from the position
of an outsider, the unevenness of the global political field, and the messiness
of human rights work—neither obscuring the political work that such
demands require, nor finding in ethics an alternative to general programs or
courses of action. They remain open and committed to the idea that the
work of justice remains ongoing: there are more demands to acknowledge
and arbitrate and different futures to imagine and work for. In their interest
in the non-finality of justice, these works, we can finally suggest, stand
against capitalism's and nationalism's normalizing of "the all-too-human sat-
edness with the demands of the distant, even when distant events are nothing but the sensational result of everyday domestic policy" (Robbins, 1999,
pp. 153–54). Conversely, in this contemporary globalizing moment, these
fictions expand our capacities for ethical agency and political action across
the shifting borders of the nation and into a cosmopolitical field.

Chapter One

# Foreign Feeling: Kazuo Ishiguro's
# *The Unconsoled* and the New Europe

Critics of Kazuo Ishiguro's bulky fourth novel, *The Unconsoled,* were quick to point out this work was only apparently different from his earlier efforts, the tight, taut novels for which he is celebrated[1]. Seemingly surreal, the novel opens with the arrival of Ryder, an internationally renowned pianist, at the gloomy hotel lobby in an unnamed European city. Initially unrecognized, he is quickly assured by the hotel clerk that Mr. Hoffman, the hotel manager, is hard at work on preparations for Thursday night; without understanding what this means, Ryder becomes aware of the sounds of a piano over the muffled noise of city traffic: "Someone was playing a single short phrase—it was from the second movement of Mullery's *Verticality*—over and over in a slow, preoccupied manner" (1995, p. 4). "Nightmare Hotel," "Sleepless Nights," and "Anxious in Dreamland"[2]—the titles of the reviews of the novel describe its unsettled mood. Listening to the porter Gustav narrate his entire professional history during an overly long ascent in the hotel elevator up to Ryder's room, Ryder realizes that they are not alone; turning, he discovers a neatly dressed young woman standing in the corner. Introducing herself as Hilde Stratmann, "a humble employee of the Civic Arts Institute" (p. 10), she alerts him to his many scheduled appointments that he cannot remember. Unable to recall the basic details about his visit to this city, Ryder encounters at every turn a person who makes new demands on him. ". . . I found myself troubled once more by a sense that much was expected of me here," he soon concludes, "and yet that things were at present on a far from satisfactory footing" (p. 26).

"Finds himself" is the verb construction *The Unconsoled* uses with regularity to describe Ryder, suggesting a belated self-recognition that is familiar in Ishiguro's first-person narrators. That Ishiguro's characters serve as shorthand for emotional repression is nowhere more evident than in a recent book review, which compares the limited emotional range of the autistic child in

9

Mark Haddon's recent novel to that of Stevens in *The Remains of the Day*[3] (Ishiguro, 1993). Despite Ishiguro's turn in "ambiance" from the Jamesian to the Kafkaesque, as Richard Rorty puts it in his review (1995, p. 13), *The Unconsoled,* it would seem, returns us to a dominant theme in Ishiguro's fiction: the sacrifice of an emotional life to a sense of professional duty. In its darkest turn, the novel suggests that Ryder, who spends his life on musical tour, in "[h]otel room after hotel room" (Ishiguro, 1995, p. 38), can no longer recognize his own home or family. The novel registers this grim fact in an early scene, when Ryder agrees to talk to Gustav's despondent daughter, Sophie. Venturing into the city's Old Town to look for her, Ryder encounters a woman who appears to know him. After Sophie introduces him, somewhat formally, to her young son—"'This is Mr. Ryder, Boris. . . . He's a special friend'" (p. 32)—Ryder hesitantly realizes that they have been making long-term plans—that they are planning, in fact, to buy a house together.

> She began to give me more details about the house. I remained silent, but only partly because of my uncertainty as to how I should respond. For the fact was, as we had been sitting together, Sophie's face had come to seem steadily more familiar to me until now I thought I could even remember vaguely some earlier discussions about buying just such a house in the woods. (p. 34)

Listening to her voice, he faintly recalls a series of arguments between them; while Sophie urges him to give up touring—"'Before you know it, Boris will be grown up. No one can expect you to keep on like this'" (p. 37)—he insists he must continue: "'You don't know what you're saying! Some of these places I visit, the people don't know a thing. They don't understand the first thing about modern music and if you leave them to themselves, it's obvious, they'll just get deeper and deeper into trouble. I'm needed, why can't you see that? I'm needed out here!'" (p. 37).

Is he? A synopsis of Part II, which begins when Ryder awakens on the second day of his visit, introduces us to the fullness of his days: after breakfast, he promises Boris that they will retrieve his favorite toy, left behind at his (perhaps their?) old apartment, but is waylaid by a request for an interview and photos from local journalists. Leaving Boris in a café with a piece of cheesecake, Ryder follows the journalists onto a tram on which he meets his old childhood friend Fiona, who tells him how disappointed she is that he didn't show up at her dinner party the night before; promising to make it up to her, he continues on his way with the journalists to the Sattler monument (more on this below). Again there is an interruption: the city's former (and now disgraced) conductor arrives at the photo-shoot, thanks Ryder for agreeing to attend a lunch meeting with local musicians, and steers him to his car. Climbing in, Ryder remembers "all at once his many other commitments for the day" (p. 187), but cannot quite extricate himself from this one. At the meeting, Ryder makes controversial pronouncements on pigmented triads and the circular dynamic in the music of Kazan; as tensions begin to flare, it occurs to him that "this café and the one in which [he] had left Boris were in fact parts of the same building" (p. 203); climbing through a narrow door into what appears to be a broom cupboard, he makes his way back to the slightly impatient child. This is not the end of the day—there is still the favorite toy to rescue, a party to attend at the Karwinsky gallery, and a dinner to eat at Sophie's apartment. But the more than fortuitous realization that he is in same café (later he will discover a dimly lit corridor that leads back from the Karwinsky Gallery to the hotel lobby) begins to reveal a psychic logic to the novel's distortedness or dreaminess; time and space, Michael Wood's reading suggests, are "governed by . . . [Ryder's] needs and worries rather than the laws of physics" (21 December 1995, p. 18). Walking with Boris back to Sophie's apartment, for instance, Ryder discovers that he and Boris can't keep up with her: "though we increased our pace, it seemed to take an inordinate time for us to reach the corner [where she turned] ourselves" (Ishiguro, 1995, p. 40). And a few pages later:

> Sophie's figure once again disappeared from our view, this time so abruptly I thought she must have gone into a doorway. . . . We soon discovered that Sophie had in fact turned down a side-alley, whose entrance was little more than a crack in the wall. It descended so steeply and appeared so narrow it did not seem possible to go down it without scraping an elbow along one or the other of the rough walls to either side. The darkness was broken only by two street lamps, one half-way down, the other at the very bottom. (p. 43)

Their evening together remains out of reach; instead, he returns to the hotel, where he believes that he "[has] one more appointment" to keep (p. 78). That these almost nightmarish dislocations are guided by his needs and worries, as Wood puts it—in this case, Ryder's anxiety about the demands of adult love—is evident in the end of Part II: after leaving dinner with Sophie rather early—"'I have a very busy morning tomorrow'" (p. 289), he tells her—he returns to his hotel room determined to fulfill his other obligations: his appointment with the mayor, his meeting with the Citizens' Mutual Support Group, and his invitation from Miss Collins to visit. " . . . [T]here could be no denying that I had been placed under some pressure" (pp. 289–90), he concludes. Throughout the novel, the city's expectations that he will help them make sense of modern music and various individuals' demands that he come to their aid interrupt his family time.

Making a familiar argument about Ishiguro's fiction, Pico Iyer asserts that Ryder has "cheated himself out of a life" by being "too accommodating, too dutiful to stand up for [his] own needs" (28 April 1995, p. 22). "[I]n honoring the little obligations," Iyer claims, "he has missed out on the biggest ones of all" (p. 22): unsurprisingly, those to his family and to himself. Against this interpretive strain, I want to suggest that these "little" obligations are not unimportant—or rather, that the novel is making a serious ethical point through their unimportance. In making this point, the novel, I will argue, alerts us to the pervasiveness of claims on us. But it also notifies us of the difficult necessity of deciding among our many pressing obligations. I will suggest that Ryder's hesitant and wavering response reflects the disturbances of the criteria used to respond to the demands made on him, reading the novel's action, which Rorty insists does not "take place against a background of real history" (1995, p. 13), into a newly uncertain Europe.

Admittedly, my first suggestion, that we validate the "little" obligations, is difficult to make. This becomes especially clear in Ryder's interactions with the porter Gustav, who makes repeated claims on him. From their initial trip in the elevator, Gustav requests his help; along with asking him to console his daughter Sophie, he also asks Ryder to mention the plight of the city's porters in his remarks on Thursday night, on which, it seems, Ryder is to perform. "' . . . [Y]ou see, sir,' Gustav says, explaining their plight, 'there's always this idea that anyone could do this job if they took it into their heads. . . . I suppose it's because everyone in this town at some point has had the experience of carrying luggage from place to place. . . . 'I'd like to do that one of these days,' [one of the city councilors] said to me, indicating the bags. 'That's the life for me. Not a care in the world'" (Ishiguro, 1995, p. 6). Like Ryder, Gustav seems to overestimate his professional and civic importance, and the results of this overestimation seem instructive. The ridiculous Porter's Dance, in which Gustav hoists larger and heavier bags while he shuffles atop a cafe table, metaphorizes to the literal point the burden of excessive demands, not least from Gustav, that Ryder undertakes:

> . . . Gustav's face remained grim with concentration, staring with enormous intensity at the strap of the golfing bag lying on the table surface. Then the elderly porter began to lower himself again, his whole body

trembling under the weight of the suitcase on his shoulder, his hand grasping prematurely for the strap still some distance below him. (p. 404)

The foolishness of this undertaking seems underscored in the exhausted end of his dance, which ultimately results in his death. But Ryder does not get the point; instead, he tries to accommodate more demands around Gustav's death: to inspect the concert piano, to pick up Sophie and Boris and bring them to Gustav—"'I'm sorry,' I said, as I turned the car, 'but I don't know my way around here so well yet'" (1995, p. 448), he insists—to convince the Hoffmans that their son Stephan really does have musical talent, to broker a reconciliation between the rehabilitated conductor, Brodsky, and his former lover, to meet with Miss Stratmann about his parents' supposed visit for his concert, and to find a decent breakfast.

These insignificant demands give new energy to Jacques Derrida's examples from *The Gift of Death*, which envisions those others to whom we are responsible as not only "one other or some other persons, but also places, animals, languages" (1995, p. 71). In this work, Derrida imagines a responsibility owed equally and unconditionally to the other—including the other as our work—and to the other others. "Duty or responsibility binds me to the other, to the other as other. . . . I am responsible to the other as other, I answer to him and I answer for what I do before him" (p. 68); but he goes on to argue, "[t]here are also others, an infinite number of them, the innumerable generality of others to whom I should be bound by the same responsibility, a general and universal responsibility" (p. 68). In the proliferating duties that Ryder takes on, the novel hints at this tension or conflict. "'You must promise me you won't let me down . . .'" (Ishiguro, 1995, p. 178), Fiona, who wants Ryder to attend her dinner party—and every other character—insists. Even at the moment of his death, Gustav, for instance, does not let Ryder out of his commitment: "'Gustav kept asking,' one of the porters reports. 'Right to the end he kept asking [if Ryder has spoken at Thursday night's concert on their behalf]. 'Any news of Mr. Ryder yet?' He kept asking that'" (p. 526). Framing ethical decisions, rather outrageously, in terms of household pets (Derrida, 1995, p. 71)—"How would you ever justify the fact that you sacrifice all the cats in the world to the cat that you feed at home every morning for years, whereas other cats die of hunger at every instant?" he asks—Derrida makes the point that the experience of ethics as impossible is an *everyday* one[4]. Emphasizing the banality of Ryder's innumerable duties, we may take this as the novel's point as well. But we may also say that the novel makes a distinction between ethics as an everyday experience of the impossible and ethics as actually impossible[5]. "Justice is beyond calculation," Drucilla Cornell argues, but "the call of the Other," like Fiona or Gustav, "is concrete" (1991, p. 116). Returning us to the ethical decision, she explains: " . . . [W]e must always calculate and participate, if we are to meet the obligation to be just" (p. 116); even as we do so, though, "we do not presume to define justice once and for all" (p. 116). The tension the novel makes felt between the singular claim and universal duty reminds us of the disjunctions Cornell identifies, and thus of the ongoing work of doing justice.

The non-finality that the novel uncovers does not mean that there cannot be a solution to the problem of multiple demands, including the demands of work and family[6]; it means that the solution will not be a fixed or permanent one. In alerting us to this non-finality, the novel holds up for scrutiny, without rejecting, Barry Lewis's firm conclusion that "Ryder's problem is that he cannot say no" (2000, p. 116). Lewis rightly notices that Ryder, "unable to turn down the demands of the people he meets" (p. 116), "is pulled in many directions at once" (p. 121). Perhaps he *should* say no to certain demands; making clear that his work is suffering, Ryder tells the hotel manager, "'Mr. Hoffman, you don't seem to appreciate the urgency of the situation. Owing to one unforeseen event after another, I haven't had a chance to touch a piano now for many days. I must insist I be allowed access to one as quickly as possible'" (Ishiguro, 1995, p. 336). Despite these exhortations, or his later realization that he has ruined his relationship with Sophie, *The Unconsoled* does not find that Ryder's professional or familial responsibilities mark the *limits* of his obligation[7]. Rather, these limits are precisely what the novel calls into question by making audible the dissonance that "results from heeding the Other whose face demands 'the equitable honoring of faces'" (Cornell, 1991, p. 116).

Iyer's claim that Ryder is cheating himself out of a life by honoring the "little" obligations is further shaken by Louis Menand's observation that Ishiguro's reputation as a psychological realist is "entirely undeserved" (28 April 1995, p. 7). "The characters in . . . Ishiguro's books are papier-mâché animations," he explains. "They don't have feelings; they simulate feelings . . ."[8] (p. 7). The flatness of his characters and the flimsiness of their internal lives are evident at the moments when they are most at stake: for instance, when Ryder discovers that his parents are not, after all, coming to hear him play. "'How much longer am I supposed to go on traveling like this?'" (Ishiguro, 1995, p. 512), he asks. In characteristically stilted prose, the novel describes his breakdown: "I collapsed into a chair and realized I had started to sob. As I did so, I remembered just how tenuous had been the whole possibility of my parents' coming to the town. I could not understand how I had ever been so confident about the matter . . ." (p. 512). Boris's heartbreak over his mother's final rejection of Ryder (a moment I will return to later) is similarly lifeless: "'But we've got to stay together, we've got to'" (p. 532). "'He'll never be one of us,' Sophie responds. 'You've got to understand that, Boris'" (p. 532). Taking seriously Menand's claim that "we are not dealing with characters and their relations 'in the traditional novelistic sense'" (15 October 1995, p. 7), *The Unconsoled,* as I see it, is far more interested in ethical experimentation than in psychological realism—and far more bracing, perhaps even unconsoling, to read as such.

The assertion that Ishiguro is not a psychological realist also puts pressure on the interpretation of the dream-like manipulations of time and space as Ryder's psychic distortions. In response to this pressure, I want to suggest that we understand these distortions as a narrative, rather than as a psychological, ploy. Like my earlier one, this is not an intuitive suggestion: the psychic logic of these distortions seems evident yet again when Ryder recognizes his hotel room as his childhood bedroom:

> It had been recently re-plastered and re-painted, its dimensions had been enlarged, the cornices had been removed, the decorations around the light fitting had been entirely altered. But it was unmistakably the same ceiling that I had so often stared up at from my narrow creaking bed of those days. (Ishiguro, 1995, p. 16)

Staring up at the ceiling or looking down at the rug, Ryder feels "once more back in [his] old childhood sanctuary. . . . All the tensions of the day—the long flight, the confusions over my schedule, Gustav's problems—seemed to fall away . . ." (p. 17). Back in his childhood room, he is safe from the demands of this visit. That it is a sanctuary from more than present difficulties becomes clear as the narrative continues. As he moves through the city, Ryder recognizes old friends from his childhood in England; Geoffrey Saunders, for one, chides him for not coming to visit when he arrived in town. Talking with him, Ryder is seized with a memory of a "crisp winter's morning in England" when, standing outside a pub "deep in the Worcestershire countryside" (p. 46), he burst into tears in front of Saunders. And when Ryder meets Fiona, he recalls her taunting him as a child about his parents' continuous arguments: "'Don't you know? Don't you know why they argue all the time?'" (p. 172). During his and Boris' trip to their old apartment complex, they run into a man who complains about the family arguments in the apartment that now stands empty—an apartment whose objects bring "a poignant nudge of recognition" to Ryder (p. 214). The neighbor explains,

"'Whenever we saw him he was sober, very respectful. He'd give us a quick salute, be on his way. But my wife was convinced that's what was behind it. You know, drink . . .'" (p. 215). He goes on to note that the father of the family tended "'to blame *her*'" (p. 215). The neighbor continues: "'Okay, he went away a lot, but from what we understood he had to, that was all part of his work. It wasn't a reason, that's what I'm saying, it wasn't a reason for her to behave in the way she did . . .'" (p. 215).

We remember that the dreamwork renders manifest, in distorted form, the latent or unconscious dream-thoughts. By means of condensation and displacement, Freud explains, the dream-thoughts are translated into the dream-content. "The consequence is that the dream-content no longer resembles the core of the dream-thoughts and that the dream gives no more than a distortion of the dream-wish which exists in the unconscious" (1958, p. 308). Suggesting the appeal of this account for literary criticism, Nicolas Rand and Maria Torok explain that "[d]ream interpretation . . . implies a form of reading that undoes distortions, expands condensations, puts displacements back in their place, and sets enigmatic visual images into comprehensible words" (1997, p. 15). Several critics uncover the secret of Ryder's childhood through this interpretive framework. Lewis concludes that Ryder, like Boris, as the above passage hints ("'it wasn't a reason for her to behave in the way she did'"), is not his father's real son (2000, p. 120); as Sophie tells Boris at the end of the novel, "'He'll never love you like a real father'" (Ishiguro, 1995, p. 532). Gary Adelman (2001) finds alcoholism as well as infidelity at the root of the family's dysfunction, surmising that Ryder's father withheld his praise and love for him. His argument undoes the distortion of the novel's many sets of silent and withholding parents and bereaved children. Between each parent and child—Gustav and Sophie, Mr. Hoffman and Stephan, Ryder's parents and Ryder, Ryder and Boris—meaningful communication breaks down. Gustav, for instance, tells Ryder that he has not spoken to Sophie since her childhood, when a "certain sad little event" (Ishiguro, 1995, p. 83), the death of her pet hamster Ulrich, occurred. Narrating the event, Gustav remembers standing at the door of her room, listening to her sob and deciding not to comfort her unless she called out to him directly. "At the center of this inconsolable place," Wood concludes, "are the unappeasable parents, the parents for whom no performance is ever good enough . . ." (21 December 1995, p. 18).

For Wood, then, the family drama gives *The Unconsoled* its title and emotional center. Here is where Freud's theory of the dreamwork is most suggestive. Understanding the dream-content as "differently centered from the dream-thoughts" (1958, p. 305), in Freud's words, I want to propose that the novel's "domestic" problem—the uncertainty over who's truly yours—is national and even international rather than familial in significance. This allows us to see differently Ryder's claim that he is an outsider to the family, and the city, where he is supposed to be at home—entering Sophie's apartment, for instance, he observes that "[t]here could be little doubt that Sophie and Boris expected me to know my way around . . ." (Ishiguro, 1995, p. 283). We witness a dynamic between engagement and avoidance in his interactions with Gustav over Sophie; as Gustav shows him around his room, Ryder decides that "for all his professionalism, for all his genuine desire to see me comfortable, a certain matter that had been preoccupying him throughout the day had again pushed its way to the front of his mind. He was, in other words, worrying once more about his daughter and her little boy" (p. 13); the memory of her despondency, Ryder decides, "was now troubling [Gustav] once more as he showed me around my room" (p. 14). That these are Ryder's worries, projected onto Gustav, is one way of reading this moment. Reading against the grain—that is, against the notion of Ishiguro as psychological realist—we may also read it as a moment of sudden and uncomfortable proximity, when boundaries become blurred and troubles shared. Ryder's response to him quickly falters; finding that he "had taken a liking to the old man and felt a wave of sympathy for him" (p. 14), he quickly backs off: "I thought about broaching the whole topic [of Sophie's despondency] with him but then . . . the weariness I had been experiencing intermittently ever since I had stepped off the plane came over me again. Resolving to take up the matter with him at a later point, I dismissed him with a generous tip" (p. 15). In fact, it is Gustav who approaches Ryder again to ask for his help in brokering reconciliation between them. Listening to his explanation of the silence between him and Sophie, Ryder feels "another wave of impatience" (p. 85): "As I keep saying, these family matters . . . I'm merely an outsider. How can I judge?" (p. 86). Expressing a similar hesitation, he says with a sigh to Stephan Hoffman, who asks Ryder to listen to him rehearse, "I'd certainly like to help you. I have much sympathy for you in your present situation. It's just that it's got so late now and . . ." (p. 149).

We may recognize Ryder's claim that he is an outsider to these "family matters"—and his resistance to deeper personal involvement—as expressive not merely of a psychic need but also of a larger historical conflict: Britain's contested relationship with Europe. British post-war politics have been characterized by disagreement, newly agitated in the early 1990s, over that relationship—from Margaret Thatcher's strident nationalism to Tony Blair's declaration that he is "*un homme d'Europe.*" Blair's assertion that Britain should be "at the center of Europe" suggests the loosening of the opposition between them, undercut but not undone by the Maastricht process, in which John Major secured British opt-outs of the European Economic and Monetary Union and the social charter which provided for labor rights—a pattern of hesitation and skepticism that typified the move toward unification. The ambivalence in British popular attitudes towards Europe is noted by Hugo Young in the widely fluctuating British approval rating for the EU, a "lack of steadiness" (1999, p. 507) that also characterizes British opinion on withdrawing from it. Writing in 1996, George Steiner observes that "[t]he notion of a European concord, except on a commercial, fiscal, or mercantile basis— and even here there is little accord—seems to recede from realistic expectation" (p. 158). The implications of this faltering are given voice to by Parkhurst, another old friend whom Ryder meets:

> When I'm out here, surrounded by these continentals, most of the time I'm fine. But now and again something happens, something unpleasant, and then I say to myself: "So what? What do I care? These are just foreigners. In my own country, I've got good friends, I've only got to go back, they'll be waiting there." (Ishiguro, 1995, pp. 327–328)

Ryder indulges this fantasy of uncomplicated allegiances and sure limits on responsibility at times. "As much as I felt deeply sorry for her," he thinks after he has missed poor Fiona's dinner party, "I found I only had the vaguest recollection of such an event having been on my schedule" (p. 176).

The wavering sympathy that is indicative of Ryder's response to these duties also indicates the moment when the criteria for making necessary ethical calculations among the many obligations facing us is put into question—that is, when it is politically difficult, and not just psychically inconvenient, to gauge closeness and connectedness. We can push further this differently centered reading of Ryder's hesitation by observing the city's own anxious Europeanness, which finds expression in one resident's lament: "Other cities! And I don't just mean Paris! Or Stuttgart! I mean smaller cities, no more than us, other cities. Gather together their best citizens, put a crisis like this before them, how would they be?" (p. 128). As Menand reads it, the novel is chiefly concerned not with personal but communal happiness, with *Gemeinschaft* (15 October 1995, p. 7); what the city has lost, he asserts, is confidence in its cultural identity. "Why don't we resign ourselves to being just another cold, lonely city? Other cities have. At least we'll be moving with the tide" (Ishiguro, 1995, p. 107). Perhaps the novel's placelessness—the characters' names and the city's architectural plan is indirectly and allusively Middle European—is a metaphor for a new global homogeneity, a grey sameness. After all, the "fakeness" of indigenous culture (15 october 1995, p. 7), as Menand puts it, is a point made both by the Porter's Dance and in its aftermath, when Ryder discovers himself, arms linked with the other patrons of the café, making up words "[he] thought sounded vaguely Hungarian" to a folk song (Ishiguro, 1995, p. 408). Yet we also feel twinges of recognition as Ryder navigates the city. As a pedestrian, he is frustrated most dramatically when he discovers a brick wall running across a city street, blocking his access to the concert hall. In an argument I return to below, Étienne Balibar reminds us that the borders of Europe, newly undetermined by the weakening of the nation-state, are haunted by their past overdetermination; the novel's wall, a sign of Ryder's own blockages in one reading, ghosts the one that focalized Europe's partition. This is not the only reference to a historically divided Europe. The Sattler monument, a "tall cylinder of white brickwork, windowless apart from a single vertical slit near the top" (p. 182), resembles what Laura Mulvey calls a "disgraced monument" (1999, p. 223), whose symbolic role has changed with the status of its referent, Max Sattler. Seeing this as a remnant of a Soviet past, we may see a post-socialist city whose multiple pasts, as Fredric Jameson says of Bucharest, are "vividly inscribed" in its various "built styles" (October 10 1995, p. 76): Old Town's squares and courtyards coexist with downtown's glassy office buildings—in Jameson's analysis, "the architecture of late-capitalism" (p. 77).

The point I want to make is not simply that the city is situated on the fault lines of Europe—between West and East, or First and Second Worlds—but that the narrative figures their present dislocation. "The street seemed much longer than I remembered," Ryder finds in his attempt to circumnavigate the brick wall, "and when I finally reached the end I found myself getting lost again in the network of little alleys" (Ishiguro, 1995, p. 389). I want to suggest that expansions and compressions of distance and space, which I earlier suggested recentered the novel's domestic content, record the new indeterminacy of Europe's borders. Ryder's discovery that the reception hall that he has driven to from the hotel is merely a corner of that hotel's atrium—that what seemed quite far is actually quite close—reminds us that the borders of Europe are "vacillating," in Balibar's words (1998, p. 217). Unfixed by the break-up of the Soviet Bloc, the reunification of Germany, and the signing of Maastricht as well as by the varied forces of globalization, they are being "multiplied and reduced . . ., thinned out and doubled" (1998, p. 220); as Balibar puts it, Europe's borders are "no longer localizable in an unequivocal fashion" (p. 219). They now stretch, he writes, "from the Atlantic to the Urals, unless it be to the Amur River, from the Nordkapp to the Bosporus, unless it be to the Persian Gulf . . ." (p. 217).

Representing the unsettling of European borders and self-understanding—as Perry Anderson explains, since the late 1980s, writers and politicians in Hungary, the Czech lands, and Poland, as well as Slovenia and Croatia, have argued that they "belong to a Central Europe with a natural affinity to Western Europe" (1997, p. 138)—this work is legible as a European Union novel, a term I adapt from Richard Eder, who has identified European Community fiction as an emergent genre (2 June 1999). Updating that generic category, *The Unconsoled* gestures to an uncertainty and anxiety over ethical response—and, pushing this reading further, humanitarian intervention—in a period of shifting, but by no means disappearing, borders: do the claims of Bosnian Muslims or Kosovar Albanians, or Chechens or Kurds, count?

Taking up the question of state intervention in Kosovo in an interview with Jim Lehrer, Tony Blair, answering questions about the use of ground troops and the extension of NATO's role, concluded that NATO could not "stand aside and let [Milosevic] conduct a policy effectively of racial genocide in a part of Europe" (Blair, 23 April 1999). But he did not acknowledge the approximately 200,000 Bosnian Muslims, Croats, and non-Serbs murdered, and the more than two million displaced from their homes between 1992 and 1995—those (or those Europeans) whom NATO decided not to help. Deepening its historical resonance, the novel evokes their displacement in the scene of Ryder's failed performance; deciding that his numerous disappointments did not "reduce at all my responsibility to all those who had waited many weeks for the moment I sat before them in front of a piano" (Ishiguro, 1995, p. 518), Ryder discovers that the auditorium's seating and the audience itself have disappeared: "Before me now was a vast, dark, empty space. There were no lights on at all, but instead, here and there, large rectangular sections of the ceiling had been removed, allowing the daylight to come down in pale shafts onto the floor" (p. 519).

Reminding us that "whether in Congo or Rwanda, Kosovo or Iraq, every intervention—and non-intervention—has its politics," Mahmood Mamdani argues that humanitarian intervention is at risk of becoming "a soothing name for unilateral and unaccountable exercises of power" if we cannot hold internationally accountable those states that wield that power[9] (26 June 2003, p. 20). His assertion offers different urgency to the argument for an agency of international law, which I take up in Chapter Two. I address the question of being personally accountable to those who may suffer the consequences of our actions there as well; here, though, I want to note the moment when the novel hints at a demand for greater accountability for the powerful and privileged actor on a transnational scale. "'It's all very well you're coming here like this,' one city member says to Ryder, '[t]hen you'll move on. It's not that simple for those of us who have to live here'" (Ishiguro, 1995, p. 370). His reminder puts pressure on Ryder's abrupt conclusion that "[w]hatever disappointments this city had brought, there was no doubt that my presence had been greatly appreciated—just as it had been everywhere else I had gone" (p. 534). As a figure of mobility and expertise, Ryder stands in for the Western subject who, working with or against the state, must recognize the effects his participation and involvement in other places may have; in a scene that may be read as another indication of his self-estrangement or as a sign of the urgency of this recognition, Ryder finds himself startled by the newspaper photos of himself in front of the Sattler monument:

> The force of the wind was causing my hair to be flung right back. My tie was fluttering stiffly out behind my ear. . . . More puzzlingly, my features bore an expression of unbridled ferocity. My fist was raised to the wind, and I appeared to be in the midst of producing some warrior-like roar. (p. 267)

Seeing himself from the local perspective, Ryder begins to wonder what the true significance of the monument is—and more generally, what the real state of affairs in this city is. As he realizes, ". . . even at this late stage, with the evening's [concert] virtually upon me, there were still certain aspects to these local issues that were far from clear" (p. 377); more pointedly, he realizes, he should have made time to meet with the local citizens' group.

The novel ends at the morning of a new day, whose dawning has stretched across the whole of the novel's final section. When Ryder first awakes at the Hungarian Cafe, after Gustav's fateful dance, the sky's "first hints of morning" (p. 413) rebuke him:

> As I went on gazing out at the square, I found myself becoming increasingly angry. I could see how I had allowed too many things to distract me from my central priorities—to the extent that I had now slept through a substantial part of this most crucial of evenings in my life. Then my anger became mingled with a sense of despair and for a while I felt close to tears. (p. 413)

One of these priorities is his relationship with Sophie and Boris, which he tries too late to repair. On a tram that circles the city, Ryder comes upon the two of them. Ryder's condolences for Gustav's death are met with a reiteration, this time from Sophie, of his position as an outsider. "'Leave us,'" Sophie says. "'You were always on the outside of our love. Now look at you. On the outside of our grief as well. Leave us. Go away'" (p. 532). It's hard to read this clumsy interchange as a painful rejection; nonetheless, we can reach the conclusion that the protagonist has, in fact, cheated himself out of a life with Sophie by being too dutiful. In Ryder's attempts to assure himself that "[t]hings had not, after all, done so badly" (p. 534), and to convince himself that he can look forward to his next trip "with pride and confidence" (p. 535), we recall Stevens, watching the pier lights go on at dusk, vowing to take up bantering and make the best of what remains of his days. But what remains for Ryder is *precisely* the entirety of this day, and the next—and their impossible fullness. The shift to early morning in *The Unconsoled* makes the conclusion that Iyer and other critics reach harder to sustain.

I do not want to suggest that the fullness of Ryder's days is simply cele-brated by the novel. For one thing, we remember Gustav's death from overexertion. We also recall Ryder's significant failures, including his failure to perform in the concert and his discovery that the audience itself has disap-peared. We may also notice the excuse Ryder makes for one of these failures (in this case, his failure to support the porters' cause): "'. . . you seem to have no idea what sort of life I have to lead. Of the vast responsibilities I have to carry. Even now, as I stand here talking to you, I'm having to think about my next engagement in Helsinki. If everything hasn't gone as planned for you, I'm sorry. But you really have no right to come bothering me like this . . .'" (p. 526). Ryder's explanation echoes the one that Rieff finds people ("versed in all the other tragedies taking place around the globe" (1995, p. 24)) offer for their shortcomings in Bosnia: "'What about Angola, Sudan, East Timor, Tibet, Haiti, Rwanda?'" (p. 24). Making a distinction between ethics as the experience of the impossible and ethics as actually impossible, the novel sug-gests that the problem of innumerable duties or vast responsibilities *is* a problem to be struggled over, not an impasse or an endpoint. That is, it alerts us to the necessity of politics in Thomas Keenan's understanding of the term: "not a solution but a struggle" (2002, p. 114).

I take the novel's emphasis, even overemphasis, on the unfinished busi-ness of justice as an invitation to renew our attention to the world rather than to turn our back on it. While I have been reading *The Unconsoled* within the context of a vacillating Europe, this invitation to continue arbi-trating commitments and making cautious determinations about what actions to take against injustice, including injustices made in the name of justice, gains more generalizing powers if we heed Bruce Robbins's call to recognize our complex and multiple belongings. Getting at the difficulty of these arbitrations and calculations in a globalizing world, he argues that we are not connected to "a" place, "simple and self-evident as the surroundings we see when we open our eyes" (1998, p. 3)—an expression that resonates in the context of this dream-like novel.

> We are connected to all sorts of places, causally if not always consciously, including many that we have never traveled to, that we have only seen on television—including the place where the television itself was manufactured. It is frightening to think of how little progress has been made in turning invisibly determining and often exploitative connections into conscious and self-critical ones, how far we remain from mastering the sorts of allegiance, ethics, and action that might go with our complex and multiple belonging. (p. 3)

Closeness and connectedness are potent forces for helping us experience and arbitrate the urgency of claims and the necessity of responding to them—a reason for making our connections to the world, including the determining and exploitative ones, more evident, as Kincaid's and Coetzee's work does. In accord with the recommendations of the above passage, I take issue with one of its injunctions, that we "master" the allegiance, ethics, and action that complex belonging requires. Putting such mastery into question, the ongoing work that *The Unconsoled* highlights exhorts us to remember that "the future is always around the corner, there is no victory, but only victories that are also warnings" (Spivak, 1995, p. xxv).

A broader generic category for *The Unconsoled* than a European Union novel is what I am calling "cosmopolitan fiction," a genre that overlaps with Paul Jay's "global fiction," which, he argues, represents and responds to the various processes of globalization (29 December 2001)—of which the European Union is an instance. I use *cosmopolitan* to stress the critical energy or contestory power of this genre that *global,* in its attachment to these seemingly inevitable processes, may not at first convey[10]. I am suggesting that in its very insistence on the unfinished, and on the everyday experience of the unfinished, Ishiguro's novel challenges one of our everyday assertions about living globally: that we cannot do enough. Or rather, its insistence challenges the complacent tone in which this assertion may be made. We remember Rieff's ventriloquism—"What about Angola, Sudan, East Timor, Tibet, Haiti, Rwanda?"—and pursue it with renewed engagement. What about them?

# Chapter Two

# Criminal Justice in Michael Ondaatje's
## *Anil's Ghost*

"She arrived in early March, the plane landing at Katunayake airport before the dawn" (Ondaatje, 2000, p. 9). The beginning of *Anil's Ghost,* in which Anil Tissera arrives in Sri Lanka from abroad, revisits the diasporic return Michael Ondaatje thematizes in his 1982 memoir, *Running in the Family.* If Ondaatje imagines himself returning to Sri Lanka as both the foreigner and "the prodigal who hates the foreigner" (1993a, p. 79), Anil purposefully refuses the notion of herself as the prodigal (2000, p. 10). While Anil reveals attachments to Sri Lanka—most notably a cross-ethnic tie to Lalitha, the woman who brought her up—the novel quickly distances itself from the memoir, which focuses on the reconstruction of a family history and a place in it. "There was a scattering of relatives in Colombo, but she had not contacted them to let them know she was returning. . . . The island no longer held her by the past. . . . Anil had read documents and news reports, full of tragedy, and she had now lived abroad long enough to interpret Sri Lanka with a long-distance gaze" (2000, pp. 10–11). The view from a distance and her stance as a visitor are formalized in her official position; traveling on a British passport with a light-blue UN bar, she returns to Sri Lanka as a forensic anthropologist for a Geneva-based human rights organization. From this opening and in her early interactions with her partner, anthropologist Sarath Diyasena, we are aware of her sense of distance or remove from Sri Lanka; "[a]fter she had left . . . at eighteen, her only real connection was the new sarong her parents sent her every Christmas (which she dutifully wore) . . ." (p. 10). Her initial remove is, in fact, important to the first point the novel makes about globalized ethics.

We gather this first point through the narrative's record of how Anil received information about the human rights violations she and Sarath have been asked to investigate. "There had been continual emergency from 1983 onwards" (p. 42), the novel notes; "Anil had been sent reports collected by the various human rights groups before leaving the United States. . . . [E]verything was grabbed and collected as evidence, everything that could be held on to in the windstorm of news was copied and sent abroad to strangers in Geneva" (p. 42). Tracing the flow of information from one place in the world to strangers in another, the novel dramatizes one of the conditions of ethics in a globalized world: we are exposed and called to respond to others in places to which we have tentative or only partially acknowledged—causal, if not always conscious (Robbins, 1998, p. 3)— connections. Anil commits herself to the ongoing work of doing justice: in the West, "[she] picked up reports and opened folders that listed disappearances and killings. The last thing she wished to return to every day was this. And every day she returned to it" (p. 42). We remember the crucial role of the portable radio in *The English Patient,* which allows Kirpal to hear of the bombing of Hiroshima and Nagasaki, reorienting his affective and ethical identifications as well as his political allegiances. Charting a more radical change in the late twentieth century, Mary Midgley asserts that "technology has hugely multiplied both the range of matters [at, I would add, a range of distances] that seem likely to concern us and our ability to affect those matters" (1999, p. 161); the discourse of human rights, she continues, can "help us select the most urgent points on which to concentrate our attention . . ." (p. 161). The discourse of human rights, in other words, can help us in the political work of negotiating among claims from people or places whose connections to us we may not have fully acknowledged—or, this novel adds, may have purposively severed.

Yet the human rights standards that Midgley suggests we appeal to are produced and applied in situations of unequal power (Robbins, 1999, p. 74); this asymmetry becomes evident in the description of the investigation Anil and Sarath head, which is arranged not only in response to complaints by Amnesty International and local civil rights groups but also, in a moment that reveals one of those causal global connections, to placate "trading partners in the West" (Ondaatje, 2000, p. 16). This is where Anil chooses to make her home: "I live here," she tells a lover when he asks about her background, "[i]n the West" (p. 36). Leaving Sri Lanka on an educational scholarship at eighteen, Anil seeks distance from her early childhood fame as an exceptional swimmer (this is the first thing Sarath mentions when they meet (p. 16)) and from the fame of her father, a physician; the novel, in fact, resists a typical diasporic reading by making migration or the severing of connection the solution to, rather than a source of, a problem (Spivak, 2001, p. 344)[1]: her circumscribed life. As the novel tells us, "[Anil] felt completed abroad. (Even now her brain held the area codes of Denver and Portland)" (Ondaatje, 2000, p. 54). Both her style of dress and her choice of virtues—anonymity and privacy (p. 72)—confirm Anil's status as a visitor, a "foreign celebrity" (p. 25), from the West; this confirmation does not discredit human rights standards or their usefulness but rather underlines the unevenness of their application[2].

In fact, Ondaatje's work makes clear that human rights violations do not happen only outside the West. His 1976 detective fiction, *Coming Through Slaughter*—whose title "sets a tone for the fiction that follows" (Updike, 15 May 2000, p. 92)—documents the various abuses (including repeated rapes by guards) that take place in the East Louisiana State Hospital, where the annual death rate reached 11 percent in the early part of the twentieth century[3]. In postmodern fashion, *Coming Through Slaughter* offers ambiguities and contingencies, gaps and pauses, rather than a resolution of its mysteries: the disappearance and eventual breakdown of jazz musician Billie Bolden. But this is not to say that it does not take a position; its final line, Bolden's pronouncement that "there are no prizes" (Ondaatje, 1976, p. 156), affirms the critical edge of the narrative: its evaluation of an unacknowledged debt to African-American cultural innovation. Adopting and adapting the conventions of the classic whodunit, the critically-minded *Anil's Ghost* refigures the "[s]o many varieties of murder" (p. 49) that characterize Bolden's lived experience in its representation of Sri Lanka's terror: people are dropped from helicopters, decapitated, burned alive. Anil and Sarath begin their investigation aboard a former passenger ship that once traveled between Asia and England (Ondaatje, 2000 p. 18), its history of movement a parallel to Anil's. On board, Sarath shows her the three skeletons he is working on, which he suspects may date back to the sixth century; what strikes Anil is a much younger bone in a pile of detritus. When Sarath tells her that the skeletons were found in a government-protected historical zone, her interest heightens; after securing a permit to work at the archaeological site, they find a fourth skeleton, which Anil suspects is a victim of a political murder, one of the "unknown extrajudicial executions" (Ondaatje, 2000, p. 18) that Sarath has described. "'This one was barely dead, Sarath, when they tried to burn him. Or worse, they tried to burn him alive.' . . . She had to wait a long time for him to say something. . . . 'Can you imagine how many bodies must be buried all over the island?' he finally asked. He was not denying anything she had said" (p. 51).

In this exchange, like the others below, we gain a sense of the tension between Anil and Sarath, which hinges on her status as a visitor or outsider—for whom the novel imagines the duties of citizenship despite and even in response to Sarath's skepticism about the Western tendency to "slip in, make a discovery and leave" (p. 44). This tension also hinges on his unclear allegiances. Recognizing the messiness of human rights work, the novel, I will argue, points to the necessity of an international framework for criminal justice, which might lend that work greater authority or power. Testing *The Unconsoled*'s emphasis on the unfinished quality of justice, the ongoing work of arbitrating commitments and calculating involvement, *Anil's Ghost* reminds us that we must always identify—and have a place to prosecute—what is unjust. I will conclude this argument with an examination of the generic conventions of detective and rationalized Gothic fiction, explaining the haunting that the novel's title describes. In an immediate sense, Anil is haunted by the voices of the relatives of victims of various abuses: as she tells Sarath's brother, the doctor Gamini, "[t]here are letters from parents who have lost children. Not something you can put aside, or get over in a hurry" (p. 133). Sri Lanka itself is a Gothic place, a cemetery, as Sarath's comments above suggest. "The country existed in a . . . self-burying motion. The disappearance of school-boys, the death of lawyers by torture, the abduction of bodies from the Hokandara mass grave. Murders in the Muthurajawela marsh" (p. 157).

John McClure's reading of *Anil's Ghost* in his chapter "*Devoti postmodernia: The religious novels of Michael Ondaatje*" is an important one; reading the novel as a story of return to religious ways of being, he maintains that the novel has political implications despite its decision not to represent the ideological components of Sri Lanka's civil war in favor of a focus on "the war's shattering effect on intimate communities, individual minds and bodies" (McClure, n.d., p. 14). Ondaatje's "restriction of focus" (p. 14) is not an elision but an evaluation of the political as it is practiced in Sri Lanka, a claim for which we can find evidence in Anil's mock toast: "'Every political opinion supported by its own army'" (Ondaatje, 2000, p. 27). Ondaatje, McClure argues, writes in the tradition of figures who "denounce war while at the same time exploring its roots in injustice and advocating non-violent forms of struggle" (McClure, n.d., 14). The novel's indictment of the predominantly Sinhalese government does recognize the origins of the civil war, which Human Rights Watch attributes to politically organized violence, part of a long pattern of state and popular discrimination against Tamils with its roots in colonial disparity[4]. An aspect of a larger interest in the postsecular projects of contemporary fiction, McClure's argument accounts for the novel's evident interest in Buddhist practice, which informs its representation of human and civil rights activism. Ondaatje's fiction is full of monks and ascetics, he asserts, whose practices chart the redemptive possibilities and political significance of retreat crucial to that practice.

Political impulses and innovations are very much in play here: one turns away from the secular for political reasons, and the new ways of life one constructs are designed to make a political difference, although not in ways familiar to those dedicated to the common secular forms of engagement. So for instance Ondaatje explores the political implications of the religious practice of retreat, giving it his strong but qualified endorsement. In these novels rich in representations of nunneries and forest monasteries, collective retreat itself becomes an essential ingredient of resistance, a way of achieving the insight, emotional balance, support, and strength necessary to do the work of healing in a violent world. (p. 3)

We see this kind of retreat in Anil's and Sarath's visit to the leaf hall, where Sarath's mentor Palipana, an epigraphist who dropped out of view after his discovery of the linguistic subtext of ancient texts was undermined, now lives. "I will not want to leave this place, she thought, remembering that Sarath had said that same thing to her" (Ondaatje, 2000, p. 97). As McClure observes, Palipana's way appeals to Sarath and Gamini as well as to Anil, all of whom "feel the lure of permanent withdrawal" (McClure, n.d., p. 17).

But McClure does not consider the conversations that take place in the leaf hall, which concern the risky work that Sarath and Anil are undertaking in their attempt to discover "if [they're] talking about a murder committed by the government" (Ondaatje, 2000, p. 89). Explaining to Palipana why he has brought him the skull of the skeleton, whom they've nicknamed Sailor, Sarath tells him that he needs an artist to recreate his face. "It is something we have to do quietly" (p. 96). McClure's emphasis on the spiritual overlooks the novel's equal attention to the secular: here, the "messy" or "untidy" conditions of socially progressive NGO work⁵. Anil embarks on this investigation without knowing exactly what Sarath's motives or allegiances are: "He was high up in the state-sponsored Archaeological Department, so how much a part of the government was he? Was he its eye and ear while assigned to aid here in the Human Rights investigation and report? In that case whom was she working for?" (Ondaatje, 2000, p. 28). At one point he asks her to turn off her tape recorder before he will speak (p. 135). Her concerns about whom she's working for, and what that work will or will not lead to, are serious, as the following passage, drawing the first of many parallels between archeological study and human rights work, reveals:

> Forensic work during a political crisis was notorious . . . for its three dimensional chess moves and back-room deals and muted statements

for the "good of the nation." In the Congo, one Human Rights group had gone too far and their collection of data had disappeared overnight, their paperwork burned. As if a city from the past had been intentionally reburied. The investigative team . . . had nothing left to do but get on a plane and go home. So much for the international authority of Geneva. (pp. 28–29)

Her frustration with the pace of the investigation is palpable: "'We're here to supposedly investigate disappearances. But I go to offices and can't get in'" (p. 44). When she protests, "'I *was* invited here,'" Sarath responds, "'[i]international investigations don't mean a lot'" (p. 45).

The novel doesn't take this conclusion, or the above ("so much for the international authority of Geneva"), as necessary ones, though. This refusal first emerges through a set of conversations and disagreements, scattered across the narrative, over the politics of truth and truth-finding that implicates Anil's status as a visitor and presses on the limits of their investigation. The first conversation takes place between Anil and Palipana, and demonstrates the similarity of their work to his: uncovering the intentionally lost or buried. Telling Anil about the kings from the historical texts he studies, Palipana draws a comparison between the exercise of power then and now:

> "We have never had the truth. Not even with your work on bones."
> "We use the bone to search for it. 'The truth shall set you free.' I believe that."
> "Most of the time in our world, truth is just opinion." (p. 102)

Sarath's beliefs echo Palipana's suspicions: "He would have given his life for the truth if the truth were of any use" (Ondaatje, 2000, p. 157). Early on, after Sarath warns Anil against being like a journalist, she confronts him: "'You have a hang-up about journalists, don't you'" (p. 44). He responds: "'That's how we get seen in the West. It's different here, dangerous. Sometimes law is on the side of power not truth'" (p. 44). During their time in the government-protected archaeological preserve, where Sailor was found, they talk again.

> "I don't know where you stand. I know . . . I know you feel the purpose of truth is more complicated, that it's sometimes more dangerous here if you tell the truth."
> "Everyone's scared, Anil. It's a national disease."
> "There are so many bodies in the ground now, that's what you said . . . murdered, anonymous. I mean, people don't even know if they are

two hundred years old or two weeks old, they've all been through fire. Some people let their ghosts die, some don't. Sarath, we can do something . . ."

"You're about six hours away from Colombo and you're whispering—think about that." (p. 53)

And during a night at the *walawwa,* the country home of a family friend of Sarath where he and Anil—joined by Ananda, the artist whom they hire to reconstruct Sailor's face—continue their work, they speak once more.

"You like to remain cloudy, don't you, Sarath, even to yourself."

"I don't think clarity is necessarily truth. It's simplicity, isn't it?"

"I need to know what you think. I need to break things apart to know where they come from. That's also an acceptance of truth. Secrets turn powerless in the open air."

"Political secrets are not powerless, in any form." (p. 259)

Without adopting Anil's "Western liberal's confidence in the power of disclosure to eradicate injustice" (McClure, n.d., p. 19), Sarath commits himself to the process of uncovering Sailor's identity and proving the government's crime, arranging to get Anil out of the country with the investigative report. Aboard the ship with the skeleton, she listens to his voice and the set of instructions on tape that Sarath has left her with. What she hears—that she must complete the report alone, that he will probably not be able to take her to the airport, that she cannot contact him again—poses a challenge to her trust in the power, or powerlessness, of secrets made public; this is not a cynical moment, though: Anil rewinds the tape. "She walked away from the skeleton and paced up and down listening to his voice again. Listening to everything again" (p. 284). These exchanges, which involve reflection on and reappraisal of political beliefs and injunctions ("the truth sets you free"; "secrets turn powerless in the open air"), ask, What else, beyond the crucial work of investigation and exposure, is available to them? What other, more formal mechanisms of accountability are possible?

The image of Anil rewinding the tape to listen again to Sarath's voice gives us a sense that she, like his brother Gamini, will remain in "permanent conversation" with him even in his absence (p. 288). In this and in the moments above we gain access to the secular in the sense that Homi Bhabha, conscious of the colonial and imperial history of the concepts of our "modern political and social lexicon" (1996, p. 203), favors: the secular as a mode of conduct rather than a specific aim, as a space of conversation and contestation (including of those aims) against which fundamentalism stands (pp. 204–5). Open to difference, to disagreement, and to risk, such a social space allows for the testing of the boundaries of and limits on choices and options. As in several of Ondaatje's novels, a certain structure—the bombed-out villa in *The English Patient* (1993b), the *walawaa* in this one—becomes the site of a strange community, situated at the edge of, and in the midst of, near ruins (the title of the second section of *The English Patient*).

Anil recognizes herself as "citizenized" by the friendship—as I have been describing it, their relationship takes the form of dialogue and self-reflection—of Sarath as well as Ananda. Before returning to the questions above, I want to pause on this recognition, which Sarath also makes, to consider how the novel imagines the extension of the political sphere. It does not do so lightly. After Sarath's sudden (and temporary) disappearance from their investigation—"[a]11 her fears about him rose again—the relative who was a minister, his views on the danger of truth" (Ondaatje, 2000, p. 269)—Anil makes her way back to Colombo; there she is forced to reconstruct their evidence in front of an audience of officials, "among them military and police personnel trained in counter-insurgency methods" (p. 271), without the skeleton, which disappears when she arrives. Rather than directly represent her argument, the novel filters the reconstruction of their evidence through Sarath, who

> in the back row, unseen by her, listened to her quiet explanations, her surefootedness, her absolute calm and refusal to be emotional or angry. It was a lawyer's argument and, more important, a citizen's evidence; she was no longer just a foreign authority. Then he heard her say, "I think you murdered hundreds of us." *Hundreds of us,* Sarath thought to himself. Fifteen years away and she is finally *us.* (pp. 271–72, emphasis in the original)

It is Sarath who most consistently articulates an opposition between the citizen and the foreign authority; earlier, he insists that she "'should live here. Not be here just for another job'" (p. 200). Anil insists that this isn't just another job; "'I decided to come back, I wanted to come back'" (p. 200). But she leaves open the question of whether she means permanently. "'. . . I could never leave here'" (p. 285), Gamini whispers to Anil at one point, but she does not make that commitment. In the openness over whether she will stay the novel acknowledges the possibility for those who do not belong to the nation to exercise what Étienne Balibar might call citizenship: the right to politics. Here, that means the right to involvement in the collective life of another country ("she is finally *us,*" Sarath concludes)[6]. Examining the disaggregation of citizenship and nationality under contemporary globalization—Anil is *citizenized* rather than nationalized—he argues, "borders have stopped marking the limits of where politics ends . . ., beyond which, in Clausewitz's words, politics can be continued only 'by other means'" (Balibar, 1998, pp. 219–20)[7]. Read in the context of this disaggregation, the fact that Anil does not, and perhaps cannot, share Sarath's and Gamini's love for Sri Lanka—"[n]o Westerner would understand the love they had for this place" (Ondaatje, 2000, p. 285)—is not a point of failing; it is not a patriotic but a cosmopolitical practice that the novel here recognizes.

In his analysis of the range of cosmopolitan practices, including long-distance nationalisms, Robbins asserts that "there is no inherent virtue in transnationality" (1998, p. 11), an assertion which resounds in the novel's suggestion that the civil war is financed by those in the diaspora. Early on, the novel acknowledges the war's "backers on the sidelines in safe countries" (Ondaatje, 2000, p. 43); later Gamini denounces "those armchair rebels living abroad with their ideas of justice . . ." (p. 132). But Robbins also calls into doubt Benedict Anderson's suggestion that there is inherent vice in transnationality, identifying in "human rights culture" and in the vocabulary around transnational NGOs emergent forms of "accountability-at-a-distance" (Robbins, 1998, p. 11). *Anil's Ghost* registers both the psychological and political seriousness of a transnational orientation. Dedicated to "the doctors and nurses, archaeologists, forensic anthropologists, and members of the human rights and civil rights organizations . . . in Sri Lanka and in other parts of the world" (Ondaatje, 2000, p. 309), the novel recognizes the toll such work can take; as one character comments, "'I got out of the Civil Rights Movement because I couldn't remember which massacre took place when and where . . .'" (p. 283). Here is where McClure's argument for the necessity of retreat registers most pointedly. For Sarath, the difference between citizen and foreign authority hinges on accountability, which Tom LeClair, in his forceful review of the novel (19 June 2000), accuses Ondaatje of lacking. In LeClair's analysis, there is no difference between the practice of Western journalists, which Sarath criticizes ("slip in, make a discovery and leave"), and Ondaatje's. In one conversation, Gamini extends Sarath's critique to Western forms of art and political writing, inviting such a comparison:

"American movies, English books—remember how they all end? . . .
The American or the Englishman gets on a plane and leaves. That's it.
The camera leaves with him. He looks out of the window at Mombasa
or Vietnam or Jakarta, someplace he can now look at through the

clouds. . . . He's going home. So the war, to all purposes, is over. . . . It's
probably the history of the last two hundred years of Western political
writing. Go home. Write a book. Hit the circuit." (Ondaatje, 2000,
pp. 285–86)

But the novel, and this is something that LeClair does not consider, does *not*
end this way. We do get a moment of Anil's desire for a less ethically and
politically engaged life; "[i]f she were to step into another life now, back to
the adopted country of her choice, how much would Gamini and the memory of Sarath be a part of her life?" . . . Wherever she might be, would she
think of them?" (p. 285), she wonders. But while Anil leaves Sri Lanka in
order to make the report public—whether she might have returned to the
"adopted country of her choice" anyway remains possible, I suggested
above—the novel does not leave with her. Its view remains on Sri Lanka,
showing us the repercussions of the report's publication in Sarath's torture
and murder, presumably by the same government forces who abducted and
murdered Sailor. "Sarath had always sidestepped violence because of his
character . . ." (p. 289), Gamini thinks, but it finds him nonetheless. The
novel reminds us, forcefully, of what remains after what Anil, now absent,
has done. It also suggests that her presence is still significantly felt: in the
final scene of the novel, half-way up the ladder he is using to repaint a Buddha's eyes, Ananda observes that "he and the woman Anil would always carry
the ghost of Sarath Diyasena" (p. 305).

A scene of private grief and one of public violence end the second-to-last section of the novel, allowing me to pursue the other mechanisms of accountability that the novel identifies a need for. Drawing up reports on the fatalities
of human rights crimes, Gamini comes upon a photo of Sarath's body, and
rushes to locate it. Following this, the narrative shifts to the successful assas-
sination of President Katugala, killed by a suicide bomber identified as "R":
"he was not just the weapon but the aimer of it. The bomb would destroy
whomever he was facing. His own eyes and frame were the cross-hairs" (pp.
293–94). The intimacy of violence in Sri Lanka—the close proximity of the
suicide bomber, the bicycle ride of blindfolded man and his captors that
Sarath once watches (p. 154)—is reversed in Gamini's stance, as he leans
over and tends to the wounds of Sarath's body. "There are pietàs of every
kind," the novel explains:

> [Gamini] recalls the sexual pietà he saw once. A man and a woman, the
> man having come and the woman stroking his back, her face with the

acceptance of his transformed physical state. It was Sarath and Sarath's wife he had witnessed, and then her eyes had looked up at him, in his madness, her hand not pausing in its stroke of the body within her arms.

There were other pietàs. The story of Savitra, who wrestled her husband away from Death so that in the startling paintings of the myth you saw her hold him—joy filling her face, while his face looks capsized, in the midst of his fearful metamorphosis, this reversal back into love and life.

But this was a pietà between brothers. (p. 288)

Ondaatje's fascination with religious figures and art may be read within the religious traditions that he venerates; it may also be read against the very divisions that such traditions may be used to support. In his analysis of the Italian artwork in *The English Patient* (1999, p. 166), Robbins aligns such artwork with a hardness and a clarity, compelling in its very transcendence of the allegiances and rivalries that Ondaatje, in this novel, does not give a full name to; the bomber's ethnic affiliation is erased. (The rivalries that he does name—sibling, sexual—are evident above.) Ondaatje accords the pietà a variety and a universality, taking this term to describe the posture of Savitra and her husband rescued from death, on the brink of a different metamorphosis from Sarath or, for that matter, Christ. In these descriptions, the novel pluralizes without discounting our conception of universality. Judith Butler, facing such a scenario, proposes as our task the labor of translation between versions or discourses of universality, which respects that the universal—our notion of the human and its possibilities, our conception of the scope of human rights—is not fully or finally achievable. To claim this is not to deny the usefulness or necessity of the category but to be open to its (unexpected) transformation (1996, p. 50).

The novel effects its own transformation on the detective novel, and, in doing so, on the universality of the law, which remains, in an urgent sense, incomplete and inadequate: "There had been years of nightly visitations, kidnappings or murders in broad daylight. . . . All that was left of the law was a belief in an eventual revenge towards those who had power" (Ondaatje, 2000, p. 56). Following Dennis Porter, we can define detective fiction as a narrative "whose principal action concerns the attempt by a specialist investigator to solve a crime and to bring the criminal to justice, whether the crime be a single murder or the endeavor to destroy a civilization" (1981, p. 5). Opening with the finding of the skeleton, the novel works as a whodunit, a mode of detective fiction that "involv[es] the tactics and strategies of putting together a coherent solution to the crime" (Pyhrönen, 1999, p. 23). In fact, it suggests that its generic status is part of a colonial literary heritage: when Anil finds Agatha Christie, P.G. Wodehouse, and Enid Blyton in the library of a rest house on the way to Bandarawela, she considers them the "usual suspects in any Asian library" (Ondaatje, 2000, p. 58). The reference to Christie, part of the "Golden Era" of British detective fiction, alerts us to certain conventions of the whodunit that the novel recalls as well as revises. "We tend to associate the classic whodunit with hermetically sealed chambers, secret passages, and remote country mansions" (2000, p. 102), David Lehman explains; the "sense of an island remoteness from which there is 'no escape' is what all the who-dunit's classic settings have in common" (p. 105). Here, of course, the island is literalized, the sealed chambers, like the archaeological site in which Sailor's skeleton is found, government-protected. But *Anil's Ghost* refuses the vision of criminality offered by the classic whodunit, in which it is "anything but the norm" (p. 110); as Sarath says at the beginning of the novel, "'The bodies turn up weekly now'" (Ondaatje, 2000, p. 17)[8].

The characteristics of the whodunit that Lehman identifies—the remote location or mansion, the sealed chambers—are also those of the Gothic. The overlap between these traditions has a long literary and critical tradition; pointing out "the obvious resemblances between explained or rationalized Gothic and detective fiction" (2000, p. 33), Marty Roth asserts that in detective fiction, "any Gothic trope—demonic beings, metamorphosis, dematerialization—is asserted to be within the limits of an expanded universe of explanation" (1995, p. 36). Historicizing detective fiction as "deeply implicated with the history of forensic technology" (1999, p. 3), Ronald Thomas notes that the detective's uncanny insight is revealed "as the simple application of a technique, or even a technology, to the variables of the present occasion" (p. 3). Both Anil and Gamini share a belief in the sixth sense (Ondaatje, 2000, p. 231). But the flash of insight that Anil has about the similarity between Sailor and Ananda, which helps identify Sailor's occupation as a miner, actually comes from her careful study of bone strictures caused by repeated stresses (pp. 178–79). As Thomas revealingly asserts, though, forensic science came to possess "virtually occult power" over the image of the human and questions of identity in modern society (1999, pp. 289–90). Terry Castle urges us to reexamine the relation between the supernatural and the rational or secular, reminding us of the origins of our metaphors and explanatory terms. Her reading of *The Mysteries of Udolpho* demonstrates that while the supernatural is apparently banished by the end of the novel, it is actually displaced "to the realm of the everyday" (1995, p. 124). Castle goes on to argue that "the most influential of modern theories of the mind—psychoanalysis—has internalized the ghost-seeing metaphor; the Freudian account of psychic events . . . is as suffused with crypto-supernaturalism as Radcliffe's" (p. 125). Freud, following the same trajectory as Radcliffe, explains the supernatural while also internalizing it: "Ghosts, for Freud, have ceased to exist anywhere but in the mind" (p. 138). The title of the novel invites an analysis of Anil's psyche. Following Sarah Brophy's reading of Devon in Jamaica Kincaid's *My Brother*, which I will turn to in the next chapter, I want to suggest that Sailor stands as Anil's "political unconscious or, as [Bhabha] argues, 'the missing person' that haunts the identity of the postcolonial bourgeoisie'" (in Brophy, 2002, p. 268). Like Devon in Brophy's analysis, Sailor "embodies her political unconscious in that he represents an extreme example of the vulnerability of those who remain in the place [she] has left . . ." (p. 269): the vulnerability of those socially and economically marginal figures, including Gunesena—whom she and Sarath find crucified on the road to Colombo, and take on as their driver—with whom she finds herself in new relation.

In poetic attempts "to see a missing person" Bhabha finds an interrogation of not only the "image of the person, but [also] the discursive and disciplinary places from which questions of identity are strategically and institutionally posed" (1994, p. 47). Ondaatje's poems from *Running in the Family* enact the same interrogation in their address to the marginal position; one represents, for instance, "the woman my ancestors ignored" (1993a, p. 87). In "The Cinnamon Peeler," which begins "If I were the cinnamon peeler," Ondaatje inhabits a conditional identification with this figure. Ajay Heble's careful reading of this poem and larger argument that Ondaatje is "attempting to provide us with a new direction for our reflection on the meaning of postcolonial belonging" (1994, p. 189) politicizes this identification, which the novel (here we remember Anil as part of "us") represents as a claim to citizenship and collectivity. Its revision of the conventions of the British whodunit, which I have begun to describe, suggests that its own literary allegiances remain contested. In his memoir, Ondaatje cites a poem by Lakdasa Wikkramasinha, "Don't talk to me about Matisse," which offers a critique "not only of European representations of non-Western culture [ironizing the memoir's paperback cover, a reproduction of a Gauguin painting] but also of a government that is perceived to have ruthlessly suppressed the spirit of a potential revolution: '*to our remote / villages the painters came, and our white-washed / mud-huts were splattered with gunfire*'" (Heble, 1994, p. 195). Ondaatje's reference to the state's suppression of the Janatha Vimukthi Peramuna (JVP) insurgency of 1971 anticipates his concerns in *Anil's Ghost*, which indicts Sri Lanka's state and security forces.

"Detective fiction ends with the embodiment of the criminal as a *graspable* object" (1995, p. 29, emphasis added) Roth concludes. *Anil's Ghost* departs from the genre on this point. The solution to the mystery of Sailor's identity and the final determination that this is a political murder is rushed and abbreviated: deliberately unsatisfying. At the third village in the insurgent area they visit, Anil and Sarath make the identification in a moment that asserts an expected connection between detective and rationalized Gothic fiction, naturalizing a supernatural figure:

> He was Ruwan Kumara and he had been a toddy tapper. After breaking his leg in a fall he had worked in the local mine, and the village remembered when the outsiders had picked him up. They had entered the tunnel where twelve men were working. They brought a *billa*—someone from the community with a gunnysack over his head, slits cut out for his eyes—to anonymously identify the rebel sympathizer. A *billa* was a monster, a ghost, to scare children in games, and it had picked out Ruwan Kumara and taken him away. (Ondaatje, 2000, p. 269)

Sarath leaves to search for his name in a list of government undesirables; two pages later, with neither Sarath's information nor the skeleton, Anil is in Colombo, presenting her evidence against the government. Making a formal accusation against the state, the novel does not represent the bringing of the criminal, in both of these cases, the state's security forces, to legal justice. Does this adhere to the conventions of the genre, which generally omit the mechanics of arrest and trial? "What is particularly notable about detective stories . . .," Porter writes, "is that they only exceptionally raise questions concerning the code: the law itself is accepted as a given" (1981, p. 121). He goes on to assert that "not only are the circumstances and motivations of the crime elided . . . but also on most occasions the spectacle of the momentous machinery of the law down to its apparatus of death . . ." (p. 123). Offering a less Foucauldian reading of the "premature closure of detective fiction" (1995, p. 29), Roth suggests that one reason for the omission of arrest and trial is the recognition that "the much-vaunted solutions . . . would not hold up in court. This damaging fact is also represented within the work when the detective knows who the criminal is but has no real evidence" (p. 29). Perhaps in Ondaatje's novel this fact is not damaging in the way that Roth imagines, revealing the fictiveness of solutions or the narrativity of truth; perhaps *Anil's Ghost*'s "premature closure" signals the fact that there is no court in which this evidence could do so. In this novel, the elision of the arrest and trial does not testify to the givenness of the law, as Porter would have it, but to its contingencies. As Anil recollects to Sarath: "'When I was in Central America there was a villager who said to us: When soldiers burned our village they said this is the law, so I thought the law meant the right of the army to kill us'" (Ondaatje, 2000, p. 44). We see as much in Sri Lanka in the novel's descriptions of human rights work: "Early investigations had led to no arrests, and protests from organizations had never reached even the mid-level of police or government" (p. 42); "'[s]ave for a few good lawyers,'" Sarath asserts, the law in Sri Lanka has been "'abandoned'" (p. 154). Identifying the limitations of the law on a national level, the novel points to the need for an international framework for criminal justice.

In its World Report for 2002, Human Rights Watch (HRW) noted the increased willingness of Sri Lankan authorities to take official responsibility for human rights atrocities, including massacres and disappearances linked to counterinsurgency campaigns. "In February [2001], the attorney general reportedly issued indictments against more than six hundred police and armed forces personnel implicated in 'disappearances' that occurred before 1994—many in connection with counterinsurgency operations against the [JVP] organization" (Human Rights Watch, 2002). As HRW asserts, however, progress on "high profile cases" was "halting or non-existent," with prosecutions stalled by defendants' petitions to move cases out of the north and east and far from civilian witnesses. "The case of five security personnel arrested in connection with the 1999 discovery of fifteen skeletons in Chemmani, thought to be those of persons 'disappeared' by the army in 1996, made little progress." Acknowledging the guidance of civil and human rights workers into "archives of terrible sadness" (Ondaatje, 2000, p. 309), Ondaatje does not point to any specific discovery as the motivation for this novel, but a resemblance to this one is clear. Prosecutions against police and security forces move slowly, if at all; HRW attested that no one had been convicted of the crime of torture since Sri Lanka ratified the UN Convention Against Torture in 1994. The organization also noted the work of local human rights organizations against official impunity and custodial abuse, as well as their involvement in international initiatives like the Durban World Conference on Racism.

As HRW concludes, the human rights movement has until recently been able "to shame and stigmatize abusive governments [and] generate diplomatic and economic pressure" against them; what they could not do was "credibly threaten [human rights criminals] with trial and imprisonment" (Human Rights Watch, n.d.) In this, and in the novel's indication of the present limitations of criminal law, we find one answer to the question about what else human rights workers need to be available to them. Proposed in

1998, the Rome Statute, now ratified by more than the necessary number of states—a number that includes neither Sri Lanka nor the US—led to the establishment of the International Criminal Court (ICC). The legacy of the Nuremberg Trials, this permanent court investigates and brings to justice rulers, public officials, and private individuals accused of genocide, crimes against humanity, and war crimes, including torture and enforced disappearances (Amnesty International, 3 June 1998). Richard Falk attributes the rekindling of the efforts to establish a permanent court to the UN Security Council's authorization of ad hoc war crimes tribunals for the former Yugoslavia and Rwanda (2000, p. 171). Articulating a distinction between a politics of human rights and a regime of effective implementation of human rights law (p. 8), he identifies the importance of "an international criminal court that is allowed to operate free from loopholes and with a sufficient independence from geopolitical oversight to make the venture [jurisprudentially] credible" (p. 9). Falk takes as a positive sign for the possibility of global justice

> the beginnings of an ethos of criminal accountability that contains no exemptions for political leaders and is being implemented at a global level under the universal rubric of punishing anyone guilty of crimes against humanity and through the moves to establish a judicial institution of global character with such a mandate. (p. 35)

I have been describing the concern with justice in a globalized world that the novel, which points to the necessity of an international justice system, makes evident. Attentive to the necessity and redemptive possibilities of spiritual retreat from the world, *Anil's Ghost* is also alert to the possibilities of secular community and cosmopolitan political practices in that world. The desire for disconnection *is* expressed by several of the characters: after the death of his wife, for instance, "Sarath had never found the old road back into the world. . . . He returned to archaeology and hid his life in his work" (Ondaatje, 2000, pp. 277–78). But through his work with Anil, Sarath, the narrative acknowledges, "had returned to the intricacies of the public world" (p. 279). Ananda, too, evidences a certain desire for remove or distance, as the final section of the novel suggests. Engaged in reconstructing an exploded statue of Buddha in the midst of continuing political turmoil—"they were finding bodies daily, not even buried, in the adjoining fields" (p. 301)—he "appeared to stare past it all" (p. 301). From the head of the statue where he and his nephew have climbed, he looks north. He sees "all the fibers of natural history around him" from "the smallest approach of a bird" to "a hundred-mile storm coming down off the mountains near Gonagola and skirting to the plains. . . . Ananda briefly saw this angle of the world. There was a seduction for him here" (p. 307). McClure finds the resistance to or rejection of disengagement enacted in the novel's final lines: "He felt the boy's concerned hand on his. This sweet touch from the world" (p. 307). We might recognize this dynamic between seduction and resistance at work in Ondaatje's plots, in which stories of love and friendship unfold against, and remain intimately bound by, political strife and crisis[9]. Registering a powerful and worldly touch, *Anil's Ghost*, in its elision of the process of arrest and trial for the criminals it identifies, alerts us to the need for a criminal court based on what Falk identifies as "an ethos of criminal accountability" that operates "under the universal rubric" of punishing such criminals.

We can take this suggestion even further: establishing a global framework for questions of justice, Ondaatje's novel poses a challenge to US opposition toward the treaty establishing the ICC, which the Bush administration has officially renounced and "unsigned." As the *New York Times* reported, ". . . the United States will simultaneously assert that it will not be bound by the Vienna Convention of the Law of Treaties, a 1969 pact that outlines the obligations of nations to obey other international treaties" (Lewis, 5 May 2002, A18). The US's campaign to persuade countries to agree not to extradite Americans for trial before the court is its latest tactic to undermine the court, which has human rights groups increasingly worried (Becker, 26 August 2002, A10). Neither these decisions nor such tactics come as a great surprise; as Barbara Crossette, summarizing a report issued by the Institute for Energy and Environmental Research and the Lawyers' Committee on Nuclear Policy, writes: "From nuclear testing and proliferation to the land mines ban to agreements on climate change to protecting the rights of women and children, over the last decade Washington has moved steadily away from accepting treaties that would be binding on the US . . ." (4 April 2002, A5). It is against such an emerging orthodoxy that *Anil's Ghost*'s cosmopolitanism stands.

Chapter Three

# Ethical Ennui and the AIDS Epidemic in Jamaica Kincaid's *My Brother*

The rhythmic and repetitive aspects of Jamaica Kincaid's prose are familiar to her readers and have been perceptively written about by her critics. Diane Simmons asserts that the intensification of both rhythm and repetition indicates an intensification of emotion, signaling both loss and grief (1994). In Kincaid's novel *Lucy*, Simmons argues, the use of rhythm and repetition accelerates around the account of the births of Lucy's three brothers, which correspond with her mother's betrayal of "her only identical offspring" (Kincaid, 1991, p. 130)[1]. In *My Brother*, which narrates the sickness and death of Kincaid's half-brother Devon Drew from complications from AIDS, this intensification expresses the affective intensity not of her mother's betrayal but of his death; this is especially evident in the final fifty pages of the text, as we note below in a passage that both describes and enacts a rhythmic, repetitive act:

> And then he died, not in the middle of the night, which was the hour he was born, but in the very early morning, at about five o'clock, the hour I was born; and I know the hour he was born because I was there, and I know the hour I was born and the hour he died because our mother has told me. And all the night he was dying, he called out over and over again the names of his brothers, and he called out for his mother. (Kincaid, 1997, pp. 170–71)

And yet this intensity, which her prose records, surprises her, as Devon has played a minor role in her life as well as in her fiction, which has focused on her love affair with her mother. Meditating on her relationship to him and the place that she is from, the work "acknowledges for the first time the significant absence of her brother from the life story she has presented" (2002, p. 266), as Sarah Brophy puts it, observing her absence from his life story as well: "I saw him when he was three years old and didn't see him again until he was twenty-one" (Kincaid, 1997, p. 149), Kincaid explains. When she is "seemingly forgotten by him in the long hours before he left the world" she thinks it is "so natural, so perfect; he was so right! I had never been a part of the tapestry, so to speak, of [his life]" (p. 175). She notes, ". . . [H]e did not know who I was, and I can see that in the effort of his dying, to make sense of me and all that had happened to me between the years he was three and thirty was not only beyond him but also of no particular interest to him" (p. 175)[2].

That Kincaid has been "cold and ruthless in regard to [her] own family, acting only in favor of [herself] when [she] was a young woman" (p. 69) is apparent in this work and the novels (*Annie John* (1995), *Lucy* (1991)) that participate in Kincaid's construction of "the autobiographical self" (Brophy, 2002, p. 268). Readers of those novels will remember the urgency and finality of the daughter's break from her mother: considering her decision to leave Antigua for England, Annie John asks herself, "Why . . . didn't I see the hypocrite in my mother, when, over the years, she said that she loved me . . ., while at the same time proposing and arranging separation after separation, including this one, which, unbeknownst to her, *I* have arranged to be permanent?" (Kincaid, 1985. p. 133). *My Brother* gives new meaning and greater context to her ruthlessness, paradoxically, by telling the story of Kincaid's discovery of an obligation to her brother, an obligation layered with familial and diasporic guilt and enabled by economic privilege. In doing so, it demonstrates that the AIDS epidemic requires not only an ethics but a politics—a politics that the work's focus on singularity helps enliven.

Describing the forces that impelled her to leave home and Antigua, Kincaid describes herself as a reluctant cosmopolitan, whose transnationalism is both "unwilling and ambivalent" (Robbins, 1999, p. 3). She recalls being sent away to help the financial crisis impelled by Devon's birth and their father's illness, revealing her former position in the international division of labor: she went to work as "a servant" for a North American family (Kincaid, 1997, p. 152), with whom she spent a summer near Chicago. (The city itself marks the distance Kincaid has traveled; she returns to it, as we will see below, as a well-regarded author having a "triumph" with one of her books (p. 156)). But in another very real sense, her transnationalism—the severance of her intimate connection with her family—is, like Anil Tissera's, entirely welcome. As we glean, her departure at age sixteen is also fueled by her vexed relationship with her mother; as Kincaid explains, at age fifteen, ". . . I was not a part of the real debacle of [my mother's] life [her sick husband and her many children], and . . . worst of all, I could not help her out of it. I insisted on reading books" (p. 132). After Kincaid's profound neglect of Devon one afternoon—rather than care for him she chooses instead to read a novel— her mother explodes in "a fury so fierce that I believed . . . that she wanted me dead . . ." (p. 131). She burns Kincaid's library, destroying "the only thing I owned in my then-emerging life" (p. 134).

Books, more than her brothers, are the objects of her childhood affections. Kincaid recalls, ". . . I would have said that I loved books but did not love [Devon] at all, only that I loved him because I was supposed to and what else could I do" (p. 129). As an adult, she remembers having neither ". . . particular feelings of affection [n]or special feelings of dislike for him" (p. 20), explaining that "I think of my brothers as my mother's children" (p. 21). For these reasons—her early preference for books, her conflicted relationship to Devon—she is amazed to discover, when she is told that he is sick and dying, "that I loved him; I could see that was what I was feeling, love for him, and it surprised me because I did not know him at all" (p. 20). Yet she proceeds to disclaim this love: "I did not love my brother, I did not like my brother, I was only so sorry that he had died . . ." (p. 106), she asserts at one point in the narrative. "I did not love him," she concludes at another, "What I felt [for Devon] might have been called love, but I still, even now, would not call it so" (p. 58). Or as she explains: ". . . my brother had died, and I didn't love him; or, at any rate, I didn't love him in the way that I had come to understand love, something so immediate . . . it was like breath itself" (p. 148). This immediacy is, instead, the way she describes her love for her husband and children. Genuinely conflicted over her feelings for Devon, Kincaid is practiced in her efforts to avoid her family's demands, which distract her from her own life: "I am so vulnerable to my family's needs and influence that from time to time I remove myself from them" (p. 20), she writes. "I do not write to them. I do not pay visits to them. I do not lie, I do not deny, I only remove myself" (p. 20). She gives an account of a colder "removal" from their lives: learning of her father's (or rather, stepfather's) death three month's after his burial ("[m]y mother and I were in one of our periods of not speaking to each other, not on the telephone, not in letters" (p. 118), she explains), she also learns of her family's destitution. As Kincaid tells it, acknowledging a mix of guilt, grief, and ruthless determination:

> . . . I felt condemned because I had so removed myself from my family
> that their suffering had gone unnoticed by me, and even as I wept over
> my father's death, I would not have done much to prevent it, and even
> as I wept over my mother's description of emotional pain and financial

deprivation, I would not do a thing to alleviate it. It was ten years after I
left my home that he died, it was ten years after he died before I saw my
home again. . . . (p. 120)

She chooses to remain in New York where she has decided to become a
writer, an undertaking her mother emphatically does not support.

The moment when she does respond to her family's needs, she, appro-
priately enough, puts down her book—now a sign of her comfortable, even
luxurious life, in which she has escaped servitude for artistry.

> At the time the phone call came telling me of my brother's illness,
> among the many comforts, luxuries, that I enjoyed was reading a book,
> *The Education of a Gardener,* written by a man named Russell Page. I
> was in the process of deciding that as a gardener who designed gardens
> for other people, he had the personality of the servant, not the personal-
> ity of the artist. . . . [W]hen the phone call rang I put the book down
> and was told about my brother.
>
> The next time I opened this book I was sitting in front of the
> Gweneth O'Reilly ward and my brother was sitting in a chair next to
> me. It was many days later. He could barely walk, he could barely sit up,
> he was like an old man. . . . It was never a great hospital, but it is a terri-
> ble hospital now, and only people who cannot afford anything else
> make use of it. (pp. 10–11)

Kincaid depicts her decision to return to Antigua and to visit the hospital,
where Devon is one of the many "who cannot afford anything else," as impul-
sive; she explains that when she heard about Devon's sickness, the "usual delib-
eration . . . —should I let this affect me or not?—vanished" (p. 20). She brings
Devon AZT and other medicines for thrush and pneumonia. The American
doctor's response to her request for a prescription for AZT—"[s]he said yes
immediately" (p. 34)—echoes the immediacy of her own response.

Confusion and even regret over her decision to help him quickly appear:
"Sometimes when I was sitting with him, in the first few days of my seeing him
for the first time after such a long time, seeing him just lying there, dying faster
than most people, I wanted to run away, I would scream inside my head, What
am I doing here, I want to go home" (pp. 22–23). And yet Kincaid reveals the
pull Devon exerts on her even after she returns to Vermont:

> . . . I talked about him, his life, to my husband, I talked about him to peo-
> ple I knew well and people I did not know very well. But I did not think I

loved him; then, when I was no longer in his presence, I did not think I loved him. Whatever made me talk about him, whatever made me think of him, was not love, just something else, but not love; love being what I felt for my family, the one I have now, but not for him. . . . (pp. 50–51)

The contrast she insists on between what she feels for him ("not love, just something else") and what she feels for her family ("the one I have now") makes the following discovery, as it does her sense of loss over his death, surprising to her: ". . . I had just discovered my brother was dying, would die, and that I did not love him, or did not recognize my feelings as love, but felt such a responsibility, an obligation to help him in some way" (p. 159).

This obligation, like her initial reaction to her father's (or stepfather's) death, is layered with complicated feelings, including guilt over her recognition that "his life is the one [she] did not have" (p. 176)—"the life that, for reasons I hope shall never be too clear to me, I avoided or escaped" (p. 176). At another point she notes that her own life is "in direct contrast to his" (pp. 166–67). But it is the relative privilege of her life that allows her to help him, she also recognizes; making clear her persistent anger at her mother, she retells the story of her mother's decision to take her out of school before she was sixteen:

My father was sick, she said, she needed me at home to help with the small children, she said. But no one would have died had I remained in school, no one would have eaten less had I remained in school; my brother would have been dead by now had this act of my mother's been all that remained of my life. . . . I would not have been in a position to save his life, I would not have had access to medicine to prolong his life, I would not have had access to money to buy the medicine that would prolong his life, however temporarily. (p. 74)

If it had been up to her mother, Kincaid thinks, she "might in fact be in the same position as [Devon] . . ." (p. 75). The recognition of what her current position allows does not blunt the resentment she also feels at sharing her privilege; she explains:

. . . [W]henever [Devon] made a special point of being with me alone it was to ask me for something I had that he wanted; earlier he had taken me aside to ask me for the pair of shorts that I was wearing; they were a pair of khaki shorts I usually wear when I go hiking in the mountains. I gave them to him, and even though I could easily replace them, I did not like giving them to him at all. I did not want them back, I wanted not to have to give them in the first place. (p. 76)

Identifying the ethical impulse of Kincaid's writing, Sarah Brophy identifies the "melancholic commitment" Kincaid makes to Devon in this work; citing Jacques Derrida, she asserts that her refusal to internalize or idealize Devon "is at the same time a respect for the other, a sort of tender rejection'" (in Brophy, 2002, p. 268). Throughout the work, Kincaid portrays Devon (and, we see above, often herself) in largely unsympathetic terms; as she recounts of one of their days at the hospital, for instance:

> . . . [W]hile we were sitting in the sun, he saw a woman wearing a pair of tight-fitting pants that outlined the curves around her pubic area, and while staring pointedly at her crotch, he said some words to her, letting her know that he would like to have sex with her ("That would fit me very nicely, you know." He said it exactly like that). She . . . would not look at him. This made me wonder at the confidence of men. There he was, diseased and dying, looking as unattractive as a long-dead corpse would look, and he would still try to convince a woman to sleep with him. (Kincaid, 1997, p. 43)

The moment in the hospital when he grabs his fungal penis and points it at her in "a sort of thrusting gesture" (p. 91)—"'Jamaica, look at this, just look at this'"(p. 91)—sharpens his repugnance to her. Her discomfort with his "diseased and dying" body, and his confident sexuality, is acute: "[e]verything about this one gesture was disorienting; . . . to see my brother's grown-up-man penis, and to see his penis looking like that. . . . I did not want to see his penis; at that moment I did not want to see any penis at all" (p. 91). She remembers instructing him to use condoms to protect himself from HIV infection, despite his assurance, another example of his bravado, "that he would never get such a stupid thing ("Me no get dat chupidness, man") (p. 8). As she later notes, he cannot say the words AIDS or HIV, referring to his illness only as "stupidness ('de chupidness')" (p. 29). The systematic bracketing of his vernacular speech marks and makes visible the social distance between them, of which she and the rest of her family remain acutely aware; Kincaid writes, ". . . [M]y mother said to me, he has gotten so black . . . (she said this to me in this kind of English, she makes an effort to speak to me in *de* kind of English I now immediately understand" (p. 9, emphasis added)[3]. But it also preserves his (often exasperating) voice; as Brophy puts it, "Kincaid refuses (by staging her failure) to speak for Devon in any language but the one she remembers him using" (2002, p. 272).

Her commitment to Devon's singularity is exercised in her attempts to describe his suffering and deterioration. Kincaid acknowledges the difficulty of using metaphors and similes to describe that suffering and deterioration, although she compares his life to the blooming and fading of a blossom (Kincaid, 1997, pp. 163, 168)[4]. But at other moments she comes up short:

> The house had a funny smell, as if my mother no longer had time to be the immaculate housekeeper she had always been and so some terrible dirty thing had gone unnoticed and was rotting away quietly. It was only after he was dead and no longer in the house and the smell was no longer there that I knew what the smell really was, and now as I write this, I cannot find a simile for this smell, it was not a smell like any I am familiar with. (p. 90)

This difficulty, here in describing the stench of his death, becomes intensified later in the text; as she writes, "when I saw my brother for the last time, alive, in that way he was being alive (dead really, but still breathing, his chest moving up and down, his heart beating like something, beating like something, but what, but what, there was no metaphor, his heart was beating like his own heart . . .)" (p. 107). These descriptions should not be read as a refusal to grant humanity to those dying from complications from AIDS but as an attempt to contend with the concreteness of his suffering. In fact, she explicitly includes Devon's experience in the common or the universal, which does not write off its specificity but allows it to stand as unmarked[5]: as she observes, ". . . the moment when [Devon] realized that "What to do" would not prevent [his dying] is a moment so universal, so common; how I wish he could have just told me, 'What to do, what to do?'" (p. 151). This inclusion achieves a more polemical force because he is not suffering from what he originally tells his family and friends—lung cancer or bronchial asthma (p. 23)—or from the traumas that Kincaid, who has internalized the particular stigmas attached to AIDS, finds more acceptable: a terrible car accident or a fatal cancer (p. 7).

"I did not take care of [Devon]," she admits, "I only visited him and took him medicines, his mother took care of him . . ." (pp. 115–16). Though she goes into debt to bring him these medicines, Kincaid is no saint. She pointedly rejects the futural promises of Christianity that her mother, assuring her that God would "bless [her] richly for bringing the AZT" (p. 72), makes; ". . . why would God suddenly enter into it now" (p. 72), Kincaid wonders[6]. More strikingly, she makes clear the limits of the responsibility she is willing to take for Devon's well-being; as we learn in the first few pages of the text, she is usually "absorbed with the well-being" of her own children (p. 7). She does so in her response to an AIDS activist who, having learned that Devon "was lying in the hospital more dead than alive . . . due to a lack of proper treatment," suggested "as if it were the most natural, obvious suggestion in the world, that I should take him to the United States for treatment" (p. 48).

> I was stunned by this, because I was doing the best I could, I have a family, I'm not rich, everybody who comes into contact with this disease knows how costly it is to deal with properly; [the activist] would have known so, how could she just say things without asking about my circumstances, without wondering what taking my brother into my life would mean to me. I said, Oh, I am sure they would not let him in, and I didn't know if what I was saying was true, I was not familiar really with immigration policies and HIV, but what I really meant was no, I can't do what you are suggesting—take this strange, careless person into the hard-earned order of my life: my life of my children and husband, and they love me and love me again, and I love them. And then she said, Oh yes, racism. (pp. 48–49)

Taking the state as her public alibi[7], Kincaid has private, and legitimate, reasons for not taking Devon into the "hard-earned order" of her life: she has a family, she is not rich. These reasons—or rationalizations—may resonate with her readers. Kincaid is defensive, but the organizer, with her too easy conclusion—"Oh yes, racism"—strikes us as pious and irresponsible; she misses or ignores any of life's complexity. (As we will see below, Kincaid rejects racism as a *sufficient* explanation for his suffering, but not out of hand.)

We can see Kincaid's recognition of the others besides Devon that she is not helping, or not helping enough, as a further test of her limits—not of what she *will* do, but of what she *can* do. Another man with AIDS dies in the hospital room that Devon first occupied, whom she thinks at first may be an old acquaintance; ". . . when I went to visit him, this Lindsay, *for I had to, no one else did,* he was being treated with the same neglect and slight and fear as my brother had been by the staff of the hospital" (pp. 136–37, emphasis added). Paralleling Devon's funeral is that of another man "with a family and not many friends; he, too, had died of AIDS. His grave was not more than twenty yards away from my brother's, and their graveside ceremonies coincided; . . . the two men were buried at the margins of the cemetery . . ." (p. 192). Hinting at the scope of the epidemic in the Caribbean, which has the highest HIV prevalence rate after sub-Saharan Africa (UNAIDS, 2002), she signals the inadequacy of what she, acting alone, can do for Lindsay, whom she feels compelled to help in the face of indifference—"for I had to, no one else did," she writes—and the other "poor and young" men and women, "not too far away from being children" (p. 32), who are suffering from AIDS-related illnesses in Antigua.

The unrelieved suffering that Kincaid observes, and in which she plays a part, also makes the point that a general or programmatic as well as a singular or individual response is required. To pursue this point I want to return to the voice of the activist to consider what politics her abrupt conclusion and the memoir itself allow. *My Brother* suggests, with Gayatri Chakravorty Spivak, that we must extend our political analysis beyond "the minimal diagnosis of racism" (1985, p. 247). There are many reasons that Devon is in the hospital; as Kincaid explains: ". . . it was not racism that made my brother lie dying of an incurable disease in a hospital in the country in which he was born; it was the sheer accident of life, it was his own fault, . . . it was the fact that he lived in a place in which a government, made up of people with his own complexion, his own race, was corrupt and did not care whether he or other people like him lived or died" (Kincaid, 1997, pp. 49–50). At other moments, she complicates, without undercutting, her conclusion that "it was his own fault," describing the culture of male sexuality in Antigua in which both local prostitution and international tourist economies play a role (pp. 39–40, 79–80). Her discovery that Devon is gay, which he has kept hidden—Kincaid wonders if the anxiety that must have characterized "the doubleness of his life . . . would have seemed to me, who knew nothing of his internal reality, as another kind of suffering, a suffering I might be able to relieve with medicine I had brought from the prosperous North" (p. 164)—evidences his own complicated feelings about his sexuality. It also gives the lie to Kincaid's assertion that Antiguans aren't "particularly homophobic" (p. 40). *My Brother* identifies what Inderpal Grewal and Caren Kaplan term "scattered hegemonies," which they enumerate as "global economic structures, patriarchal nationalisms, 'authentic' forms of tradition, local structures of oppression and legal-juridical oppression on multiple levels" (1994, p. 17). As we can see in the following passage, the text acknowledges a non-nationally bounded conjuncture of political and economic determinations that contribute to Devon's situation:

> The reason my brother was dying of AIDS at the time I saw him is that in Antigua if you are diagnosed with the HIV virus you are considered to be dying; the drugs used for slowing the process of the virus are not available there; public concern, obsession with the treatment and care of

members of the AIDS-suffering community by groups in the larger non-AIDS suffering community does not exist. There are only people suffering from AIDS, and then the people who are not suffering from AIDS. It is felt in general, so I am told, that since there is no cure for AIDS it is useless to spend money on medicine that will only slow the progress of the disease; the afflicted will die no matter what; there are limited resources to be spent on health care and these should be sent where they will do some good, not where it is known that the outcome is death. This was the reason why there was no AZT in the hospital; but even if a doctor has wanted to write a prescription for AZT for a patient, the prescription could not be filled at a chemist's; there was no AZT on the island, it was too expensive to be stocked, most people suffering from the disease could not afford to buy this medicine. . . . (Kincaid, 1997, pp. 31–32)

This passage identifies the various cultural narratives that imagine those living with AIDS as the irretrievable victims of an "implacable" disease; Steven F. Kruger argues that the reliance on such narratives explains the lack of focus on issues of treatment, on lobbying for the improvement of the lives of those with AIDS (1996, p. 80)[8]. It also describes the economic marginalization of Antigua, its inability to afford the drugs its citizens require. Observing the rhetoric of the passage, we can identify a certain gap or pause between these explanations; Kincaid begins the passage with a catalogue of several reasons that Devon is dying of AIDS, and goes on to note that "even if a doctor had wanted to write a prescription for AZT for a patient, the prescription could not be filled at a chemist's . . .; it was too expensive to be stocked" (Kincaid, 1997, p. 32). Is local indifference aligned meaningfully or coincidentally with Antigua's economic marginalization? Kincaid isn't sure. Another way to ask this question is: do the scattered hegemonies that Grewal and Kaplan describe line up with, overlap, or conflict with one another? One conclusion that can be drawn from this passage is that the global field of political action is uneven (Spivak, 1991, p. 177): commitment to one concern may not (though it also may) be the answer to another. This does not mean giving up on multiple concerns but rather giving up on the convenience of the single issue, which is, for Spivak, "merely the shortest distance between two sign-posted exits" (p. 177). As Grewal asserts, recognizing the plurality of feminisms, "there is not one, agreed-upon 'subject of feminism' that is to be forged. . . . There are as many subjects of feminisms as there are feminisms . . ." (Grewal & Kaplan, 1994, pp. 236–37). This notion of unevenness elaborates on the conception of cosmopolitan citizenship that

Ondaatje's novel develops, asking us to take into account the multiple subjects of a necessary politics, which demand action on and not easily across the scales of the local, the regional, and the global.

In the face of the refusal of the single issue, the commitment to the singular and the contingent and to the specific demands and possibilities of the situation, paradoxically, may *sharpen* a political program, calling for the testing and the refinement, not necessarily the rejection, of assumptions, generalizations (like "racism"), and predictions. We can see the above passage, which, like Kincaid's failed metaphors for Devon's suffering body or her experience of his death—"if it is so certain, death, why is it such a surprise. . . . Why is it so new, why is this worn-out thing, death, someone dying, so new, so new?" (Kincaid, 1997, p. 193)—expressing such a commitment. A further and related reason to engage in such a process of "reappraisal" (Attridge, 1994, p. 76) emerges out of the insistence Grewal and Kaplan make on the ongoing questioning (again, not necessarily the abandoning) of feminist narratives "in order to avoid creating new orthodoxies that are exclusionary and reifying" (1994, p. 18)[9]. In their insistence on this questioning, Grewal and Kaplan confirm Stuart Hall's assertion that "certainty stimulates orthodoxy, the frozen rituals and intonation of already witnessed truth . . ." (1996, p. 45).

Against such orthodoxy, Kincaid's narrative suggests that anti-racism is not an adequate or supple enough political stance. Racism will not do for those within or outside the borders of Antigua confronting the sexual traffic in women, latent or manifest homophobia, the lack of political will, unfair drug pricing, and entrenched poverty, as recent political successes suggest. Since the publication of *My Brother,* the price of antiretroviral drugs, and more specifically of the triple "cocktail" or therapy patented by multinational pharmaceutical companies, has been successfully challenged by the manufacture and sale of generics; under public pressure, these companies have lowered drug prices. UNAIDS reports that the principle of preferential pricing for AIDS drugs has been accepted by the pharmaceutical industry; as its 2002 report on the epidemic details, countries' rights to invoke compulsory or voluntary licensing has been affirmed by the WTO. As the *New York Times* reported, fifteen Caribbean nations are now able to buy medicine as a group (rather than as individual countries) from six pharmaceutical companies at steep discounts though, as the article also noted, these prices remain high for most Caribbeans living with HIV or AIDS (Associated Press, 7 July 2002, p. A4). What has shifted over the last years, according to Tina Rosenberg (writing in January 2001), is the sense that AIDS in poor countries is untreatable; she observes the important efforts of Brazil and articulates the need for a further global commitment, which she argues for in more than

reasonable or pragmatic terms; not only the security of the globe and the via-
bility of the African continent, which public discussions often center on, but
also the suffering of the still untreated demands it.

Rosenberg also notes that despite claims that lower prices and looser
patents will negatively affect research and innovation, "the drug companies'
argument is in essence a defense of high profits" (28 January 2001, p. 58);
their efforts, she argues, have been "slow, grudging, and piecemeal" (p. 28).
What she helps identify, and what Kincaid's text also observes, is the ethical
passivity that capitalism encourages or promotes. Kincaid does not exempt
herself from capitalist society; at a book reading in an independent bookstore
in Chicago, she feels a kinship with the owner, "who had her own worries
about the ruthlessness of capitalism and the ruthlessness of the marketplace
. . . and the ruthlessness of life itself, and though she never did say this, I
gathered . . . she meant her own worthiness made her exempt from all this,
marketplace, capitalism, life itself; I was sympathetic, since I feel exactly that
way about my own self . . ." (pp. 156–57). Nonetheless, giving a reading,
trying to sell books, she is engaging in the activities of the marketplace (the
desire of writing and publishing a book is, after all, that people will buy it
(p. 156)); not exempting herself from the workings of capitalism, she does
not exempt herself from its tolerances: in her "now privileged North American way" of living, she is "full of pity at the thought of any destruction, as
long as [her] great desires do not go unmet in any way . . ." (p. 125). She
goes so far as to insist that when she learned of Devon's death, ". . . I wished
something else was happening, I wished I was complaining about some lux-
ury that was momentarily causing me disappointment: the lawn mower
wouldn't work, my delicious meal in a restaurant was not at an ideal temper-
ature . . ." (p. 178). No longer simply a strategy for self-preservation, ruthlessness becomes a condition and effect of capitalism itself.

We find a deepening record of "ethical ennui," which Bruce Robbins
describes as integral to the nationalist project[10], in Kincaid's framing of the
crisis that is Devon's life and the emergency that is the AIDS pandemic in
terms of unequal standards of living, apparent in the passage above, and
unequal access to medical care. She exposes the discrepancy between these,
maintained, she suggests below, by a willful ignorance, in an instance that
both adds onto ("but then this") and intensifies our perception of the
unavailability of the AZT that Devon urgently requires:

> But then this: one night my brother had a terrible headache and needed
> something to ease the pain; there was no aspirin on the ward where he

was staying and no aspirin in the dispensary. A nurse on duty had some in her purse for her own personal use and she gave my brother two of them. There are people who complain that a hospital in the United States will charge six dollars for a dose of Tylenol; they might wish to look at this way of running a hospital: bring your own medicines. (p. 34)

That Kincaid *can* bring Devon medicines otherwise unavailable to him underscores the discrepancy between North and South.

As I write this, much is being made of capitalism's failures of "conscience" and "character"—the second term used in a *New York Times* editorial (7 July 2002) by Jean Strouse (the biographer of J.P. Morgan)—in light of the accounting scandals that have shaken Wall Street. Those who have proposed certain regulatory schemas to guarantee both conscience and character seek to defend capitalism only to and for its domestic participants: the ordinary investors and American stockholders who have been hurt by these scandals. Nowhere in these conversations about "conscience" is mention made of those outside the nation's borders (or the workers inside those borders) who suffer bodily, environmental, and even spiritual degradation. Perhaps the treatment of this scandal points to the limitations (which is not to say the irrelevance) of rationalized moral standards, which, Drucilla Cornell reminds us, are often used "to give us a reason for not heeding the call of the Other" (1995, p. 84). After all, if we meet these standards (not actively misrepresenting our profits, for example), we are living moral lives; what else is required of us?

That a certain moralism attaches to Devon's and Lindsay's suffering, a moralism that might license ethical non-response or political inaction, is the final point I want to make before turning to Kincaid's relationship to the place she visits from. As Kincaid reports at one moment, "I missed seeing [Devon] suffer. I missed feeling sorry that I could see him in his suffering, I missed seeing him in the midst of something large and hoping he would emerge from it changed for the better" (Kincaid, 1997, pp. 57–58). Revealing the basis for her dissatisfaction with his unproductive life, she states, "Nothing came from him: not work, not children, not love for someone else" (p. 13)[11]. Yet within the memoir a critical stance toward such moralism begins to emerge, despite the contrast that Kincaid draws between Devon and another unnamed brother who eulogizes him at his funeral. Though the entire text might be read as an extended eulogy for Devon, it also provides an account of the one given, and the one not given, at his funeral.

[T]his brother said a few words about his dead sibling, the one he had named "Patches," but he did not mention that, the part about the name Patches, he only recalled that Devon loved to play cricket, how close they had been when they were schoolboys together; he did not say how afraid they were when their father . . . died and they did not want to attend his funeral and hid from our mother . . . ; he did not say how his dead brother's carelessness with his own life might have led to such an early death and was a contrast to his own caution and industriousness (he held three jobs: an accountant, a peddler of imported foods in the market, and a bass-steel-drum player in the most prominent steel band in Antigua). (pp. 194–95)

Drawing a moral distinction between Devon's carelessness and her other brother's caution and industriousness, she goes on to observe that she and he mourn for Devon in the full knowledge that even if "cured of his disease he would not change his ways" (p. 195). Her conclusion that "nothing good could come of him being so ill . . ." (p. 21) needs to be read in this context, articulating a stance against the morality of suffering, and perhaps against the implicit morality of AIDS itself.

I want to sharpen this critical or oppositional edge of *My Brother*, taking into account not only what Kicaid is writing, but also whom she's writing to, which becomes explicit in the final pages. *My Brother* does not end with the eulogy for Devon but rather moves, somewhat unexpectedly (though we should note the book's dedication to Ian "Sandy" Frazier, a long-time contributor to *The New Yorker*), into one for William Shawn. He is the late editor of that magazine, the publisher of her first fiction (the stories that compose *At the Bottom of a River* (1983)), and the father of her husband. Their relationship parallels Kincaid's relationship to the place she has made her home—not Vermont specifically, but the metropolitan center at which Shawn stands. As she explains,

> For many years I wrote for a man named William Shawn. Whenever I thought of something to write, I immediately thought of him reading it, and the thought of this man, William Shawn, reading something I had written only made me want to write it more. . . . [T]he point wasn't to hear him say he liked it [and this is significant; see below] . . . but only to know that he had read it, and why that should have been so is beyond words to me right now, or just to put it into words (and it was only through words that I knew him) would make it not true, or incomplete,

like love, I suppose. . . . Almost all of my life as a writer, everything I
wrote I expected Mr. Shawn to read. . . . (pp. 196–97)

Shawn is dead, a situation that seems to change her life as a writer; she
decides, however, that she will write "about the dead for the dead" (p. 197).
"The perfect reader has died, but I cannot see any reason not to write for
him anyway, for I can sooner get used to never hearing from him . . . than to
not be able to write for him at all" (p. 198). She continues to write to the one
who, in Derrida's words, is "no longer living, no longer there, who will no
longer respond" (1996, p. 1), but whose response she can imagine.

Moving from the margins of a cemetery in Antigua to the cultural center of New York and to the eyes and ears of Shawn seems to recreate Kincaid's
upward mobility; as it continues, it reveals the opposite of a desire for
fatherly approval or bland assimilation:

> . . . [W]hen I first heard of my brother dying and immediately knew I
> would write about him, I thought of Mr. Shawn, but Mr. Shawn had
> just died, too, and I had seen Mr. Shawn when he was dead, and even
> then I wanted to tell him what it was like when he had died, and he
> would have not liked to hear that in any way, but I was used to telling
> him things I knew he didn't like, I couldn't help telling him everything
> whether he liked it or not. . . . I thought, . . . this will be the end of any-
> thing I shall write for Mr. Shawn; but now I don't suppose that will be
> so. (Kincaid, 1997, p. 197)

In this passage we gain insight into a dynamic that we can trace through her
writing for his magazine. In the introduction to *Talk Stories,* a collection of
pieces she wrote for *The New Yorker,* Kincaid explains that "[u]ntil I wrote
about the West Indian Day carnival in Brooklyn, I had appeared in the Talk
of the Town section . . . as a person who said interesting things. Not long
after that, I began to write my own contributions to the Talk of the Town. I
wrote in the 'We' voice and I did not like it a bit at first and then I did not
like it altogether" (2001, p. 11). Her incorporation into the "we" is also an
alteration of that voice, as the pieces on daytime dancing and Miss Jamaica,
among others, demonstrate. If she feels constrained by the "we," she uses it
to press ideas about America, coolness, and cultural homogeneity; one piece,
which begins "[s]ince we haven't been to Antigua in more than ten years"
(2001, p. 67), features a conversation with a woman who notes the presence
of American popular culture in Antigua, undercutting the coherency of the
"Folk Experience" (p. 18) that white spectators at the West Indian parade

seek out. Kincaid signals the disturbance she causes to the metropolitan center in her ongoing insistence—this will not be the end of what she will write
for him—on telling Shawn "things I knew he didn't like."

Like *Lucy, My Brother* answers no to the question, "does cosmopolitanism from the margins leave the center precisely as it was?" (Robbins,
1999, p. 101)[12]. Published by Farrar, Straus, and Giroux, one of the most
literary of publishing houses, the memoir brings the international—the
AIDS crisis as it is lived in Antigua—"into the intimacy of metropolitan
space" (Robbins, 1999, p. 112). Homi Bhabha describes the process of
introducing the global "into the very grounds—now displaced—of the
domestic" (1996, p. 202) as one of vernacularization[13], giving new significance to the bracketing and preservation of Devon's speech. I want to suggest that *My Brother* itself figures as an act of vernacularization. *My Brother*
reveals the global as part of the local, now displaced; claiming a history that
makes the metropolis possible (Spivak, 2001, p. 352), both Kincaid and
Devon consider "the thing called history . . . an account of significant triumphs over significant defeats recorded by significant people who had bene-
fited from the significant triumphs" (Kincaid, 1997, p. 95). As Kincaid
writes, "he thought (as do I) that this history of ours was primarily an
account of theft and murder ("Dem tief, dem a dam tief") . . ." (p. 95). Kincaid also demonstrates that the reasons Devon is dying of AIDS cannot be
separated from the ways of living that the profit-driven political and corporate leaders and passive members of "the prosperous and triumphant part of
the world" (p. 101) practice. The work transforms our sense of what is local
and what is global—but not to "the dereliction of . . . representation,
responsibility or judgment" (Bhabha, 1996, p. 202).

The work ends on an affirmative note. On its final page, Kincaid
thanks the doctors and the pharmacist in Vermont for prescribing and making medicine available to Devon despite the fact that "[t]hey did not know
him" (Kincaid, 1997, p. 200). Pointing out the importance of the singular
act, *My Brother,* I have suggested, also points to its inadequacy—and to the
necessity of a politics that learns from singularity, even as it rejects the single
issue. Bonnie Honig suggests another term for politics in a global field: democratic cosmopolitanism, which takes among its goals "the generation of
actions in concert across lines of difference" (2001, p. 13). Seeking to root
this cosmopolitanism, she asks at one point, "what if we redeployed the
affective energies of kinship on behalf of a democratic politics that is more
cosmopolitan than nationalist in its aspirations?" (p. 72). Honig finds such
an example of this in the model of sister-cities, which "are not limited 'to carrying out a single project,' and this makes them an important complement

to more temporary, issue-oriented forms of local and international solidarity [ . . . ]" (p. 72). In Honig's example, we find another way to suggest that *My Brother*, evidencing the unrelieved suffering in the Caribbean, generates practices of citizenship that exceed both state boundaries and the single issue: by bringing Devon, the difficult younger brother, into the intimate space of the metropolis.

Chapter Four

# History Is Larger than Goodwill:[1] Restitution and Redistributive Justice in J. M. Coetzee's *Age of Iron* and *Disgrace*

In an interview with Tony Morphet, J. M. Coetzee once wondered "whether it isn't simply that vast and wholly ideological superstructure constituted by publishing, reviewing and criticism that has forced on me the fate of being a 'South African novelist'" (Morphet, 1987, p. 460). Yet his work undeniably concerns South Africa.[2] One of the problems with reading it in *national* terms may be that such reading fails to recognize the global histories and international networks that it thematizes and belongs to—in part through its South African-ness, which lends it greater marketability, as Coetzee's own comments suggest. More precisely, such reading fails to recognize that national histories are global. Homi Bhabha suggests that we might see Coetzee as a part of a new literary and cultural internationalism, which resists the denial of "the complex interweavings of history, and the culturally contingent borderlines of modern nationhood" (1994, p. 5)[3]. These historical interweavings and borderlines are addressed by *Age of Iron* and *Disgrace,* published just over a decade apart, which concern the dismantling of apartheid and the reconstruction of South Africa; as I read them, they participate, as literature, in a discussion about what Elazar Barkan (2000) sees as evidence for the growth of an international ethics and as a mechanism of economic justice: restitution.

Taking the form of a letter, *Age of Iron* opens not with a salutation but with a direct address: "There is an alley down the side of the garage, you may remember it, you and your friends would sometimes play there. Now it is a dead place, waste, without use, where windblown leaves pile up and rot" (1998, p. 3). It is in this alley that the letter's writer, Mrs. Curren, comes upon a homeless man, Vercueil, who has arrived with his dog on the day she has been diagnosed with terminal cancer; she considers this diagnosis "not good" but also "not to be refused" (p. 4). "Two things, then, in the space of an hour: the news, long dreaded, and this reconnaissance, this other annunciation. The first of the carrion birds, prompt, unerring. How long can I fend them off? The scavengers of Cape Town. . . . Cleaners-up from after the feast. . . . My heirs" (p. 5). What emerges in the novel's opening pages is Mrs. Curren's sense that she is out of time: not only is she at the end of her life, but she is going to be superseded or overrun. This sense—not entirely unwelcome (the diagnosis is "not to be refused")—also finds expression in her description of herself as one of "the children of that bygone era," who, "[i]f justice reigns at all, . . . will find [themselves] barred at the first threshold of the underworld" (p. 92); as she writes, "[w]hite as grubs in our swaddling bands, we will be dispatched to join those infant souls whose eternal whining Aeneas mistook for weeping" (p. 92). Revealing her professional identity as a former professor of Classics, her reference to Aeneas also marks a cultural affiliation and a colonial identification. In "What Is a Classic?" Coetzee asserts that "the feeling of being out of date, of having been born into too late an epoch, or surviving unnaturally beyond one's term . . . is a not uncommon sense of the self among colonials . . ., particularly young colonials struggling to match their inherited culture to their daily experience" (2001, p. 6). This also describes the experience of the old colonial, witnessing the deterioration or dismantling of her cultural position. "This car is old, it belongs to a world that barely exists anymore [from when, as Mrs. Curren later says, "British was best" (p. 99)] but it works. What is left of that world, what still works, I am trying to hold on to" (p. 71); later she admits, "'I am letting things run down'" (p. 93). Is she, as Helen Small suggests of David Lurie, the protagonist of *Disgrace,* writing herself out of the future[4]? That this is a desire she both entertains and resists is clear when she imagines checking herself into the hospital: "what a relief it would be to give myself up to [a nurse's ministrations] now! . . . [W]hat is it that keeps me from yielding?" (Coetzee, 1998, p. 70). But it is the fact of the letter itself, made possible by the arrival of Vercueil and the affront he poses to her carefully arranged life—he stands in opposition to her values of industriousness and cleanliness, yet she acknowledges that "in the look he gives me I see myself in a way that can be written" (p. 9)—that suggests otherwise. The letter or papers, which she asks him to mail after her death, suggests that she is writing herself, quite literally, *into* the future.

  She is, in fact, going to die—and this death will be part of my argument for the passing on that the letter achieves. It is written to her self-exiled daughter in America, who has promised not to return to South Africa: ". . . all I can give her, all she will accept, coming from this country" (pp. 31–32). Transmitting more than she knows, the letter/novel allows its readers—and we might see her daughter figuring the international address of the work— to meditate not only on the asymmetries and inequalities between worlds, as

Bhabha asserts of Coetzee's fiction, but also on their necessary redress. The novel recognizes not only a singular but also a historical responsibility, giving voice to a demand for Western restitution and the ongoing work of redistributive justice for the dispossessions of African land and livelihood under colonialism and apartheid, which is also a demand for a more equitable future. One of the questions I will ask in the second part of this chapter is, what happens to this demand in Coetzee's novel *Disgrace,* which negotiates South Africa's re-entrance into an increasingly globalized capitalist economy (Attridge, 2000)?

The parallel between Mrs. Curren's condition and that of the Afrikaner state, both at the onset of collapse, is clear to her; she writes at one point, "[i]t was like living in an allegory" (Coetzee, 1998, p. 90). As Dominic Head points out, the inscription "1986–89," printed on the final page of the novel, locates its action in the key years of anti-apartheid struggle, in which black resistance "found a focus in the activities of an increasingly militant youth, and in a new wave of school boycotts" (p. 131). The novel also references what human rights groups called "the war against children," waged by the South African government and its security forces; in its findings, the Truth and Reconciliation Commission (TRC) concluded that between 1960 and 1994 "the greatest proportion of victims of gross human rights [violations] were youth, many of them under eighteen" (1998, p. 254). We see this war and South Africa's various deformations in the state-sponsored murders of Bheki, the son of Mrs. Curren's live-in domestic, and his friend "John," who arrive at her home after the schools in Guguletu have been closed. Bhabha asserts that in the fiction of Nadine Gordimer and Toni Morrison, and, I would add, Coetzee, "the recesses of domestic space become sites for history's most intimate invasions" (1994, p. 9). The challenge that John poses to her authority—"Must we have a pass to come in here" (Coetzee, 1998, p. 47), he asks, tauntingly, of her backyard—confirms this point. If "in the old days" he "would have been destined to be a garden boy and eat bread and jam for lunch at the back door and drink out of a tin" (p. 151), John stands now as one of the children of the times, "at home in the landscape of violence" and this age of iron (p. 92).

Derek Attridge has written strikingly on what the presence of John in Mrs. Curren's home provokes[5]. Throughout the novel, he notes, "we are made to feel the acute difficulty of establishing any relations across the divide between bourgeois white liberal and committed black revolutionary" (1994, p. 73); he observes that her "opposition to his political beliefs is not distinct from her dislike of him as a person" (p. 73). As she admits after visiting John in the hospital, where he has been taken after being hit by a police van and where she lectures him (to no response) on Thucydides, "I would rather I had spent myself on someone else" (Coetzee, 1998, p. 79). Yet she struggles to respond to him when he shows up unexpectedly at her home from the hospital; as she laments to her daughter,

> My dearest child, I am in a fog of error. The hour is late and I do not know how to save myself. As far as I can confess, to you I confess. What is my error, you ask? . . . I cannot touch it, trap it, put a name to it. Slowly, reluctantly, let me say the first word. I do not love this child, the child sleeping in Florence's bed. I love you but I do not love him. . . . My heart does not accept him as mine: it is as simple as that. In my heart I want him to go away and leave me alone. (p. 136)

Her language reveals her self-understanding as a mother; "[w]hen they are in trouble they come to a woman" (p. 135), she thinks after making John a sandwich and putting him to bed. Yet this self-understanding is also challenged by her attempt to come to terms with him, as he is precisely *not* her own. We can see the disturbance this attempt causes: "[n]ot wanting to love him," she wonders, "how true can I say my love is for you?" (p. 137). In her insistence that she "must love . . . this child" (p. 136), is Mrs. Curren trying to redefine love—as something that stems from, rather than stands in opposition to, duty, as Attridge suggests (1994, p. 75)—or duty itself? I think we can say duty, rereading her insistence that she must love him as an expression of that duty. By naming her duty to him *love,* she suggests the urgency of establishing with him what Gayatri Chakravorty Spivak often calls by that name (that is, love): ethical singularity. To inhabit such a relation means seeing John neither as a person who must adopt her values nor as a person for whom she must have unqualified admiration (Spivak, 1998, pp. 340–41), but as a person whom she must struggle to engage with and learn from. Her record of his and the other voices of those she disagrees with most suggests this struggle, as does her attempt to imagine herself in John's position: most notably, in her live-in maid's bedroom, where he barricades himself with a gun, and waits for the police to storm the door.

> I am here in my bed but I am there in Florence's room too, with its one window and one door and no other way out. Outside the door men are waiting, crouched like hunters, to present the boy with his death. In his lap he holds the pistol that . . . was his and Bheki's great secret, that was going to make men of them; and beside him I stand or hover. The barrel of the pistol is between his knees; he strokes it up and down. He is listening to the murmur of voices outside, and I listen with him. (Coetzee, 1998, p. 175)

The sexualizing of his relation to the gun, which he strokes between his legs, marks the otherness she is trying to engage. Her grim conclusion that the gun represented his manhood also marks her unwillingness to concede to it.

Through her interactions with the police, whose arrival to her backyard stages another historical "invasion" into the space of the domestic, Mrs. Curren recognizes not only a singular but also a historical responsibility, which are, of course, linked. When she hears the first shot, she runs ("I did not know I had it in me" (p. 151)) to the window of the room, and tries to convince him to come out; she is unsuccessful, and he is killed while still inside. The police came, she realizes, "to defend me, to defend my interests, in the wider sense" (p. 153). "'A crime was committed long ago. How long ago? I do not know. But longer ago than 1916, certainly. So long ago that I was born into it'" (p. 164). Looking past the year of her birth, she extends the framework of injustice beyond Afrikaner rule, which she also excoriates: "Legitimacy they no longer trouble to claim. Reason they have shrugged off. . . . Sitting in a circle, debating ponderously, issuing decrees like hammer blows: death, death, death" (p. 29). "'Though it was not a crime I asked to be committed, it was committed in my name'" (p. 164), in the name, that is, of the European or the West. Driven outdoors by the murder, she tells an indifferent Vercueil, who continues to allow her a kind of self-reflection, that the crimes of both colonialism and apartheid had a price.

> "That price, I used to think, would have to be paid in shame: in a life of shame and a shameful death, unlamented, in an obscure corner. I accepted that. . . . What I did not know, *what I did not know*—listen to me now!—was that the price was even higher. I had miscalculated. Where did the mistake come in? It had something to do with honor, with the notion I clung to through thick and thin, from my education, from my reading. . . . I strove always for honor, for a private honor, using shame as my guide. As long as I was ashamed I had not wandered into dishonor. That was the use of shame: as a touchstone, something that would always be there, something you could come back to like a blind person, to touch, to tell you where you were. . . . I have been a good person, I freely confess to it. I am a good person still. What times these are when to be a good person is not enough! . . . What I had not calculated on was that more might be called for than to be good." (pp. 164–65)

We should note that her turn to religious language is not underwritten by a belief in God (pp. 137–38). What this "confession" reveals is what is called for in these times (another indication that she is not writing herself out of them) is more than she can figure by the moral standards of shame and honor, the legacy of the Western tradition she embodies. Perhaps the term *price,* which implies a determination that she reveals herself inadequate to, is the incorrect one. Diane Elam argues that the historical obligation to the other—in Mrs. Curren's case, to the African or the non-white—is a debt that exceeds full calculation and yet must be repaid, albeit without the "final solace of redemption" (1994, p. 111); this debt, Elam notes, cannot be "wash[ed] away" by goodwill (p. 110). It is not enough to be good, Mrs. Curren asserts, "'[f]or there are plenty of good people in this country'" (Coetzee, 1998, p. 165).

Mrs. Curren's recognition of the need for restitution emerges from the partial sight or insight that she gains, which does not culminate in a final illumination. I will trace this emergence in the next few paragraphs. Samuel Durrant (1999) proposes that Coetzee's early work makes blindness, politically necessitated and culturally managed, visible; in a departure, *Age of Iron* illuminates what she has not been able to see, as well as what it means not to. With a social realism we are unused to in Coetzee, the third chapter, which takes us into Guguletu, vividly dramatizes the burning of the township by *witdoeke,* or state-sponsored vigilantes. With Florence and her cousin (or perhaps her brother), Mr. Thabane, Mrs. Curren watches the "scene of devastation: shanties burnt and smoldering, shanties still burning, pouring forth black smoke. . . . Gangs of men were at work trying to rescue the contents of the burning shacks . . . or so I thought till with a shock it came to me that these were not rescuers but incendiaries . . ." (Coetzee, 1998, p. 95). She can only tell Mr. Thabane that what she sees is terrible. "'It is not just terrible,'" he argues, "'it is a crime. When you see a crime being committed in front of your eyes, what do you say?'" (p. 98). Mrs. Curren bears witness to an injustice that, in its scale, exceeds her: "'To speak of this'—I waved a hand over the bush, the smoke, the filth littering the path—'you would need the tongue of a god'" (p. 99).

Narrating the episode in Guguletu, she quotes from the account Freud tells of the sleeping father who, dreaming of his child who lies dead in the next room, fails to awaken to save his corpse from burning: "'Father, can't you see I'm burning?' implores the child, standing at his father's bedside. But his father, sleeping on, dreaming, did not see" (p. 110). In *Unclaimed Experience,* Cathy Caruth observes that "the dream takes its 'moving' power . . . from the very simplicity and directness, the burning of his child's body that the father sees through his sleep" (1992, p. 94). Charting the shift in the emphasis in interpretations of this dream, Caruth understands awakening as "an appointment with the real" that "occurs not merely as a failure to respond but as an enactment of the inevitability of responding . . ." (p. 105). The dream's pathos, then, comes not only from the loss of the child but also from the fact that it is the child who commands the father to awaken and to survive "no longer simply as the father of a child, but as the one who must tell what it means not to see" (p. 105). Looking at Bheki's body—the bullets inside which, according to Mr. Thabane, would read "Made in South Africa. SABS [South Africa Bureau of Standards] approved" (Coetzee, 1988, p. 103)—Mrs. Curren thinks, "[n]ow my eyes are open and I can never close them again" (p. 103); soon after she asks, "[h]ave I ever been fully awake?" (p. 109). In Caruth's reading, the awakening is, above all, an act of transmission, "handing over the seeing it does not and cannot contain to another (and another future)" (1992, p. 111)—an act of transmission materialized in Mrs. Curren's letter, which will, she realizes, reveal more than she knows: "attend to the writing, not to me" (Coetzee, 1988, p. 104).

Telling what it means not to see, she describes the life she has lived as a doll's life (p. 109); yet she also wonders if "[i]s it given to a doll to conceive such a thought" (p. 109). Reframing a remembered photograph of her family taken in her grandfather's garden, she reveals both the occlusion and the occluded:

> There are flowers behind us that look like hollyhocks; to our left is a bed of melons. . . . But by whose love tended? Who clipped the hollyhocks? Who laid the melon seeds in their warm, moist bed? Was it my grandfather who got up at four in the icy morning to open the sluice and lead water into the garden? If not he, then whose was the garden rightfully? Who are the ghosts and who the presences? Who, outside the picture, leaning on their rakes, leaning on their spades, waiting to get back to work, lean also against the edge of the rectangle, bending it, bursting it in? . . . No longer does the picture show who were in the garden frame that day, but who were not there. (p. 111)

Materializing their presences, she reveals the gardeners who made her grandfather's and her own life (and even the "civilization" that Mr. Thabane directs her back to from Guguletu (p. 107)) possible. The photograph captures or condenses a European history of seeing the land, of which Mrs. Curren is partly self-conscious[6]. Coetzee is entirely so. Rita Barnard writes that his *White Writing* "illuminates the crucial, embarrassing blindness implicit in the white man's dream about the land" (1994, p. 49), a dream that supports or enacts the erasure of the black man "as the farmer of an earlier age, or the agricultural worker, or even just as human presence" (p. 49). We can see this

visual history in the account *White Writing* gives of the first European settlement "planted" (1988b, p. 1) in 1652 at the Cape of Good Hope.

> It was set there for a specific and limited purpose: to provide fresh pro-
> duce to East Indiamen trading between the Netherlands and Asia. The
> Dutch East India Company, which ran the settlement, had little interest
> in the hinterland of the Cape, which, report said, was barren, inhos-
> pitable, and sparsely peopled. . . . For the next century and a half, till
> the colony became a pawn in the great-power rivalry of Britain and
> France, the Company tried, irresolutely and unsuccessfully, to discour-
> age the spread of settlement into the interior, to hold the colony to what
> it had originally been planned as: a trading post, a garden. (p. 1)

Through the photograph—of a garden, the primal scene of South Africa's
entry into a global economy, the latest forms of which *Disgrace* will consider—Mrs. Curren uncannily restores black Africans to land from which
they have been originally and multiply dispossessed ("no longer does the
picture show who was there, but who wasn't there"). Implicitly answering
her question, "whose was the garden rightfully?"—and here we can remember Mrs. Curren's earlier assertion that in the old days, John would have
been a "garden boy"—the novel alerts us to the necessity and urgency of
white or Western restitution for the legacy of colonialism extended under
apartheid.

Mahmood Mamdani evokes this history in his critique of the partial
truths of the TRC, which, by focusing on gross human rights violations ille-
gal under apartheid itself, missed most of its victims. I want to cite this critique in order to investigate another impulse towards redistribution that the
letter exhibits and extends. Noting that the law establishing the TRC asked
it "to frame the gross denial of rights after 1960 within a historical context,"
he asks,

> Is not that context a history of conquest and dispossession . . .? An
> understanding of gross violations that would have included the vio-
> lence done to 3.5 million victims of forced removals, and an under-
> standing of context that would have highlighted the colonial violence
> leading to the dispossession of land and the militarization of labor,
> would have produced a different kind of truth. It would have illumi-
> nated apartheid as a reality lived by the majority, a reality that produced
> racialized poverty alongside racialized truth, both equally undeserved.
> (Mamdani, 2000, p. 180)

The violence of apartheid, he argues, was not just about "defending power by denying people's rights. . . . [I]ts aim was to dispossess people of means of livelihood" (p. 179). Exposing the racialized truths of South Africa, the novel confronts the reality of living under racial capitalism. Having driven Florence to meet her husband, known as William, Mrs. Curren watches him at work.

> His job was to pounce on a chicken, swing it upside down, grip the struggling body between its knees, twist a wire band around its legs, and pass it on to a second, younger man. . . . This was William's work. . . . For six days of the week this was what he did. . . . Or perhaps he took turns with the other men and hung chickens from hooks or cut off heads. For three hundred rand a month plus rations. A work he had been doing for fifteen years. So it was not inconceivable that some of the bodies I had stuffed with bread crumbs and egg yolk and sage and rubbed with oil and garlic had been held, at the last, between the legs of this man. . . . (Coetzee, 1998, pp. 41–42)

The passage continues by contrasting the beginning of William's day, which starts at 5 A.M., to that of Mrs. Curren, still asleep at that hour: drawing a link between them, this passage demonstrates her own place in the division of labor. It is a recognition she can't quickly dismiss: "At least it is not cattle he is slaughtering, I told myself. . . . But my mind would not leave the farm, the factory, the *enterprise* where the husband of the woman who lived side by side with me worked . . ." (p. 44, emphasis in the original). She goes on: "I thought of all the men across the breadth of South Africa who, while I sat gazing out of the window, were killing chickens, moving earth, barrowful upon barrowful; of all the women sorting oranges, sewing buttonholes. Who would ever count them, the spadefuls, the oranges, the buttonholes, the chickens?" (p. 44). In these reflections she confronts what Mamdani considers the link between racialized power and racialized privilege (Mamdani, 2000, p. 179).

Addressing the question of fulfillment, David Attwell replies to Benita Parry's claim that "Coetzee's fiction is marked by the absence of a 'transfigured social order'" (Attwell, 1998, p. 173). Against this claim, he asserts that *Age of Iron* does "allusively give positive content to certain ethical propositions" (p. 176); working "around the denial of reciprocity that seems entrenched in colonial relationships," it projects "the possibility of an ethical community in a society which has historically shown little propensity to achieve such a state" (p. 177). I suggested above that the "positive content" of the novel is reparative; here I want to consider another version of fulfillment through Drucilla

Cornell's argument that if the other calls us to responsibility we cannot easily determine when we have met it, that is, when we have done enough[7]. Not only John but also these workers call Mrs. Curren to such responsibility: "my mind would not leave the farm, the factory." Cornell's argument does not offer an invitation to cynicism but to recommitment and ongoing effort; if justice is beyond calculation—who could ever count these acts of mechanized labor, Mrs. Curren asks—Cornell reminds us that "we must calculate, participate if we are to meet the obligation to be just" (1991, p. 116). The novel's premise, as a letter to be sent on after death—and thus a gesture and commitment to the future, rather than a suspension of time (Attwell, 1998, p. 175)—extends the same invitation to ongoing effort, within the context of the above passages, to reassessing the racialized distribution of benefits.

Mrs. Curren takes notice of disparities of wealth not only on the scale of the national (after the death of Bheki she writes out a check to Florence) but also the international. As she tells Vercueil, she cannot go stay with her daughter because she cannot afford to die there; "'[n]o one can, except Americans'" (Coetzee, 1998, p. 76). She revisits this disparity at the end of the novel; looking at a picture of her grandchildren on a lake in the United States, she thinks: "The line runs out . . . in these two boys, seed planted in the American snows, who will never drown, whose life expectancy is seventy-five and rising. Even I, who live on shores where the waters shallow grown men, where life expectancy declines every year, am having a death without illumination. What can these two poor underprivileged boys . . . hope for?" (p. 195). They are precisely not poor and unprivileged except in the terms that might matter most: having some idea of what happens or has happened in South Africa (this writing ". . . has taken me from where I have no idea to where I begin to have an idea" (p. 194), she notes). She wonders if her daughter, reading the letter, will cast it away from her: "*This is what I came here to get away from, why does it have to follow me?*" (p. 194, emphasis in the original). Mrs. Curren's desire to disown these two boys ("they are too distant to be children of mine of whatever sort" (p. 195)) is met with a desire to claim Vercueil (and his dog) as her family (p. 195). Bruce Robbins might describe this turn from her family to Vercueil as a kind of disassembly and reassembly of identity, required, he argues, by international feminism, human rights, and environmentalism (1999, p. 171). The novel also charts such a disassembly in her preparations for death: "Letting go of myself, letting go of you, letting go of a house still alive with memories: a hard task, but I am learning" (Coetzee, 1998, p. 130). As I suggested at the beginning of this discussion, however, she is not letting herself off the hook.

From Mrs. Curren's own reflections on her American reader, I want to address the larger question of what the letter/novel, if anything, passes on. To answer this we might look to Bhabha's assertion, which I cited above, that Coetzee's novels, "documents of a society divided by the effects of apartheid," enjoin the international community "to meditate on the unequal, asymmetrical worlds that exist elsewhere" (1994, p. 5). The move "from the specific to the general, from the material to the metaphoric" (p. 5), he argues, "is not a smooth passage of transition and transcendence" (p. 5); rather, the "'middle passage' of contemporary culture, as with slavery itself, is a process of displacement and disjunction that does not totalize experience" (p. 5). I want to suggest that such a passage from the material to the metaphoric is represented in the novel's final moments, in which Mrs. Curren narrates her own death. "I got back into bed, into the tunnel between the cold sheets. The curtains parted; [Vercueil] came in beside me. . . . He took me in his arms and held me with a mighty force, so that the breath went out of me in a rush. From that embrace there was no warmth to be had" (Coetzee, 1998, p. 198). Her passage (recorded by her own hand) from life into text allows the narrative to achieve a more generalizing power, to orient our thinking towards the persistent, or persistently maintained, asymmetries between worlds and also, as she has done, towards their necessary redress. Bhabha insists that such a passage is not a transcendence of particulars or the totalization of experience, which the dates that close the novel ("1986–89") also suggest.

Bhabha helps me make the point that the terms of restitution and redistribution will need to be worked out in and for specific situations, to address particular histories and demands. What *Age of Iron* attests to, in its representation of Mrs. Curren, is the willingness of a middle-class, or, as she prefers, "bourgeois" (Coetzee, 1998, p. 150) individual to confront her own benefits or profits from a system—be it apartheid or capitalism or their unholy union—that seems much larger than her. Their loss is not something that David Lurie in *Disgrace* specifically mourns (though at one point he does recall what was possible, or what power was available to him, "in the old days" of apartheid (Coetzee, 1999, pp. 116–17))[8]. He does, however, criticize the "campaign of redistribution" (p. 176). Returning us to the material from the metaphorical, *Disgrace* represents one (or at least one) version of the working out of restitution, narrating a South Africa that has not lived up to *Age of Iron*'s demands.

The corporatizing of the university is one moment in *Disgrace* that points to South Africa's re-emergence into the global economy after the end of apartheid; readers, especially academic readers, will immediately take note of the transformation of the professional identity of David Lurie from professor of modern languages to adjunct professor of communications. According to Anthony O'Brien, this reentrance has meant the normalization of the nation's political economy; observing the shift from a redistributive policy to neoliberalism, he identifies the interests that help produce this shift as both foreign and local capital, which seek to "preserve the structural inequalities of South African racial capitalism that oppress the everyday lives of black working people" (O'Brien, 2001, p. 4). Arguably, O'Brien continues,

> even after giving full credit to the reforms under way in infant mortality and other primary health care, electrification, the water supply, housing, and land claims, these inequalities are being remedied in the new regime in an ameliorative rather than a structural fashion and show fewer signs of any sweeping structural remedy now that the acceptance of neoclassical economic orthodoxy by the ANC in its macroeconomic program known as GEAR (Growth, Employment, and Redistribution)—under pressure from local and international capital—will continue to prevent it. (p. 4)

He sees this shift to the right reflected in Nadine Gordimer's *The House Gun* (published in 1998, one year before *Disgrace*), whose domestic plot, he asserts, represents her narrower focus and modest aspirations for post-apartheid South Africa. The house gun (or, in this case, farm gun) figures in *Disgrace* as well; Ettinger, the neighbor of David's daughter Lucy, offers to lend them one after the brutal attack on them on her smallholding in the Eastern cape: three men (one is really a boy) gain entry into her house, lock David in the bathroom, and gang-rape Lucy. As Ettinger tells them, "'I never go anywhere without my Beretta'" (Coetzee, 1999, p. 100). O'Brien concludes that Gordimer's novel indicates that "the victory of the gun is a warning to return to the book" (2001, p. 266)[9]. Does *Disgrace* also reflect this rightward shift? What does *it* have to say about the importance of the book?

David's comments on "the great campaign of redistribution" (Coetzee, 1999, p. 176) help answer this first question.

> A risk to own anything: a car, a pair of shows, a packet of cigarettes. Not enough to go around, not enough cars, shoes, cigarettes. Too many people, too few things. What there is must go into circulation, so that everyone can have a chance to be happy for a day. That is the theory; hold to the theory and to the comforts of theory. Not human evil, just a vast circulatory system. . . . Cars, shoes, women too. There must be some niche in the system for women and what happens to them. (p. 98)

We are to read David's comments as a caustic reflection on what has happened to them (and on a later burglary of his apartment). Yet we also recognize the caustic tone as the novel's own. The first part of the novel, with its campus scenes of David in front of a sexual harassment board, "reads, unusually for Coetzee, as satire" (Attridge, 2000, p. 103)[10]. As the novel makes clear in the transformation of David's professional identity, part of the university's "great rationalization" (Coetzee, 1999, p. 3) and in the renaming of the university as Cape Technical University, the model of the university has become corporate[11]. Part of a global transformation, as Attridge notes, David's courses, Communications 101 and Communications 201, evidence the shift to understanding students as consumers and learning as the acquiring of skills that will facilitate students' entry into the global workplace. What is being criticized in the first part of the novel is the reduction of the university and its functions to the bottom line: "Like all rationalized personnel, he is allowed to offer one special-field course a year, irrespective of enrollment, because that is good for morale" (p. 3). If we apply this criticism of the logic of the bottom line to David's comments above, we gain access to a critique of restitution as an exchange of goods—and even, to use the terms *Age of Iron* makes available, as goodness—rather than a reform of structural inequalities, which both local and international capital have reason to maintain[12].

The question of how women "fit into" such a system of redistribution is one that Lucy herself raises; first insisting that the rape is a private matter, she later asks, "'What if . . . what if *that* is the price one has to pay for staying on? Perhaps that is how they look at it; perhaps that is how I should look at it too. They see me as owing something'" (p. 158). It's not Lucy but David who historicizes her response not to press charges; as he surmises, "'You want to make up for the wrongs of the past, but this is not the way to do it. If you fail to stand up for yourself at this moment, you will never be able to hold your head up again'" (p. 133). As he asks her, "'Do you think that by meekly accepting what happened to you, you can set yourself apart from farmers like Ettinger? . . . Is it some sort of private salvation you are trying to work out? Do you hope you can expiate the crimes of the past by suffering in the present?'" (p. 112). Lucy specifically rejects the terms of salvation (which is not to make her reasoning less opaque or less problematic; more on this below). Earlier, the novel rejects the language of the theological for the purpose of coming to terms with past abuse, as is evident in its satiric treatment of the harassment hearing[13]; David is asked to make a confession (p. 51) (one member of the committee asks, "'Have you consulted anyone—a priest, for instance . . . ?'" (p. 49)), and to offer a statement "'[i]n the spirit of repentance'" (p. 58). He is right to reject such language for this purpose for "'repentance belongs to another world, to another universe of discourse'" (p. 58). As he puts it later, "'[t]his is the only life there is'" (p. 74). But what does this mean for Lucy?

I don't think the novel gives us much insight into Lucy or why she refuses to press charges or leave the farm; she claims that she is not doing this for the reasons David thinks. "'I am not just trying to save my skin'" (p. 112), she tells him; "'[y]ou keep misreading me. Guilt and salvation are abstractions. I don't act in terms of abstractions'" (p. 112). This lack of access is emphasized by David's inability to identify with her: "[h]e can, if he concentrates, if he loses himself, be there, be the men, inhabit them, fill them with the ghost of himself. The question is, does he have it in him to be the woman?" (p. 160). The novel does show us that the kind of accommodation she understands herself making is a patriarchal one; explaining her decision to give up her lease to her neighbor Petrus, conspicuously absent during the attack and now housing one of the assailants, she tells David: "'I have no brothers. I have a father, but he is . . . powerless in the terms that matter here. To whom can I turn for protection? To Ettinger? It is just a matter of time before Ettinger is found with a bullet in his back. Practically speaking, there is only Petrus left'" (p. 204). Through its characters' identification of restitution with a position of subjection—which Lucy, agreeing to stay on under these circumstances, cannot be exempted from[14]—the novel points to what Spivak might call gendering perceived as ethical choice (which Mrs. Curren's invocation of love should not be read as; it is, I suggested, a means by which she names a singular responsibility to one who is precisely not her own). Reactions to the novel (the following is Athol Fugard's) point to the same: "We've got to accept the rape of a white woman as a gesture to all of the evil that we did in the past? That's a load of bloody bullshit. That white women are going to accept being raped as penance for what was done in the past?" (in Attridge, 2000, p. 99).

The question that remains, however, is whether the novel perceives this as an ethical choice. Does it endorse such a posture of subjection or subjugation? We might think so when David finally returns to the farm to find Lucy, now pregnant from the rape, and thinks that "[w]ith luck she will last a long time, long beyond him" (Coetzee, 1999, p. 217). I think what the novel makes clear, however, is that hers is no kind of choice at all: it is, as Lucy herself realizes, a way of accommodating to patriarchal forms of social organization, into which David fits. This accommodation is also visible in the terms in which Melanie, the student with whom David has an affair and almost rapes, makes herself available to him; when she shows up at his house one evening and asks, arranging herself in her underwear on his daughter's bed, if she can stay with him, he wonders, "Mistress? Daughter? . . . What is she offering him?" (p. 27). Such a position or posture is also a way of accommodating to an accelerating capitalism, a point that can be made by looking to the woman who opens the text. At the beginning of the novel, David's solution to "the problem of sex" (p. 1) is a weekly visitation to Soraya, a Muslim woman, whom he hires from an escort agency. "For a ninety-minute session he pays her R400, of which half goes directly to Discreet Escorts. It seems a pity that Discreet Escorts should get so much. But they own No. 113 and other flats in Windsor Mansions; in a sense they own Soraya too, this part of her, this function" (p. 2). We can conclude from these examples that the solution to gendering perceived as ethical choice is not the abandonment of ethical thinking but the interrogation of that gendering and what maintains it.

David's question about Lucy—does he have it in him to be the woman?—is much the same question he puts to himself when working on a chamber opera about Byron and his mistress Teresa. "Can he find it in his heart to love this plain, ordinary woman? Can he love her enough to write a music for her?" (p. 182). The opera unexpectedly takes voice in the cries of a middle-aged Teresa to her dead lover, wandering "among the shades" (p. 182). "Teresa leads; page after page he follows" (p. 186). Michael Marais finds the Orpheus myth thematized throughout *Disgrace,* and takes it as figure for creation itself; he describes writing as an Orphic descent in which the writer is affected by and rendered responsible for an ungraspable alterity (2000). Marais, however, misses the Orphic encounter that surprises David in the midst of composition. "Then one day there emerges from the dark another voice, one he has not heard before, has not counted on hearing. From the words he knows it belongs to Byron's daughter Allegra; but from where inside him does it come? *Why have you left me? Come and fetch me!* calls Allegra. *So hot, so hot, so hot!* she complains in a rhythm of her own that cuts insistently across the voices of the lovers" (Coetzee, 1999, p. 186). The cry echoes that of the child—"Father, can't you see I'm burning"—in *Age of Iron* and reminds us of the tradition in which he is at home. But this unhomely moment—her voice emerges from the dark— also figures the act of being open, or being opened, to an unexpected voice. This is true not only of the solitary act of writing, suggested by this scene, but also of the study of literature; perhaps this scene also encourages us to pay attention to the other girls in the novel, those whom David cannot quite hear.

In telling the story of a man confronting the waning of his sexual attractiveness—considering Lucy's pregnancy, David wonders, "[w]hat pretty girl can he expect to be wooed into bed with a grandfather?" (p. 217)—the novel taps into a larger trade or traffic in women, returning us to the question of South Africa's global position. After Soraya's exit from his life, he returns to the agency and is asked, would he like an introduction "to another of our hostesses? Lots of exotics to choose from: Malaysian, Thai, Chinese, you name it" (p. 8). Deepening the echo of the global trafficking of women, the greatest number of whom are from Asia, that the naming of these "exotics" suggests, David gives as his occupation "'[e]xport-import'" (p. 8). We sense his predilection for the exotic in his interest not only in Soraya but also in Melanie, with her "almost Chinese cheekbones [and] large, dark eyes" (p. 11). If her youth is striking, even to him—"the women he is used to are not as young, as perfectly formed" (p. 30)—she is not the only young one that he seeks out:

> The streetwalkers are out in numbers; at a traffic light one of them catches his eye, a tall girl in a minute black leather shirt. . . . They park in a cul-de-sac on the slopes of Signal Hill. The girl is drunk or perhaps on drugs: he can get nothing coherent out of her. Nonetheless, she does her work on him as well as he could expect. Afterwards she lies with her face in his lap, resting. She is younger than she had seemed under the streetlights, younger even than Melanie. He lays a hand on her head. The trembling has ceased. He feels drowsy, contented; also strangely protective. . . .
>
> The girl stirs, sits up. "Where are you taking me?" she mumbles.
> "I'm taking you back to where I found you." (pp. 194–95)

As this final sentence suggests, she comes from nowhere and anywhere; the traffic in girls, mostly from Angola and Mozambique but also from other African and Asian countries, reflects not only the myth that sex with virgins will prevent AIDS but also the increased demand of foreigners for sex with children (BBC News, 23 November 2000). The novel makes the point with Spivak that the globalization of the traffic in wealth, "dissolving even the proper name"—both prostitutes he hires from the escort service are called Soraya—is "not an overcoming of the gendered body" (Spivak, 1993, p. 95). *Disgrace* points to the need for analysis in the way that she envisions it: we must think not only about how the world has abandoned Africa but also about what it finds there (Spivak, 1998, p. 337); South Africa, for instance, has become a destination for sex tourism. This is the same kind of analysis demanded by what Spivak calls the "successful pimping" for transnationals of women into sweated labor by ethnic entrepreneurs and by the forced competition engineered by the World Bank and the World Trade Organization (pp. 336–37).

As Spivak writes, "history is larger than personal goodwill, and we must learn to be responsible as we must study to be political" (p. 337). In this context, learning to be responsible means becoming transnationally literate (p. 337), learning the histories of the World Bank and other international agencies that map the world's investment boundaries. "As the barriers between fragile national economies and international capital are being removed," she argues, "the possibility of social redistribution, uncertain at best, is disappearing even further" (p. 338). *Disgrace* observes South Africa's entrance into the global economy with a critical eye; we might take this observation further to conclude that its critical stance towards the reduction of the university, and South Africa's social and economic policy, to the logic of the bottom line evidences Coetzee's *critical* cosmopolitanism. Taking up the question of white or Western responsibility for African dispossession acknowledged by *Age of Iron*—a responsibility that is larger than goodwill, as that novel attests—*Disgrace* suggests to us that redistribution is endangered by furthering the cause of global capitalism. The novel, as we have seen, resists the too-easy conclusion that the world has abandoned Africa, revealing instead the new opportunities for the exploitation of women. Bhabha suggests that the transnational histories of migrants and refugees, "these border and frontier conditions" that the sex workers, as ambivalent or coerced cosmopolitans, inhabit in and around Cape Town, may form the new terrains of world literature (1994, p. 12). Following Spivak, he also seeks to "world" literary works, as I have tried to do for these two novels. As literary texts, *Age of Iron* and *Disgrace* have the power to hold open the possible (Gibson, 1999, p. 16); we can see in their approach to historical responsibility a commitment to what remains, in Spivak's words, "uncertain at best."

Afterword
# "To touch the future on its hither side"

In Part Six of Kazuo Ishiguro's *When We Were Orphans* (2000), which takes place in Shanghai in October 1937, detective Christopher Banks leaves the city's International Settlement. After fleeing a rendez-vous with his would-be lover, he takes a bewildering car ride into the Chinese areas of Shanghai, seeking the house where he suspects his long-missing parents are to be found. One way to read this novel is as yet another study of a painfully deluded character who allows his work (and his childhood traumas) to sabotage any chance he has for love or romance, and thus for a truly meaningful life. However, in the midst of the novel—after his spurning of his lover and before the recognition, made after rereading one of her letters, of the emptiness of his life (pp. 334–36)—we come upon an encounter that offers another possibility for relation, and for meaning[1]. This is the significance of Part Six. Unable to reach the house by car, Christopher seeks assistance in a nearby police station, complete with broom cupboards that give access to observation towers. From the tower he can see what the Chinese police lieutenant calls "the warren," where the factory workers live in "houses with tiny rooms, row after row, back to back" (p. 251); it is through this that he will need to travel to get to the house. To Christopher, making his way through this "ant's nest" (p. 251), the slum district seems "a vast, ruined mansion with endless rooms" (p. 258); it represents another version of Darlington Hall[2]. The gothicness of this space—a quality that we may identify in *The Unconsoled*'s dark corridors and maze-like tunnels as well—is emphasized in his travels through it: behind various walls and from different rooms come terrible cries that he finds both eerie and transfixing (p. 261).

The eeriness is intensified in the encounter on which this section of the novel hangs. Groping his way through "this ghastly terrain" (p. 254), Christopher enters a large space, bathed in the reddish glow of a lantern. There were a lot of people standing about in the shadows. . . . I had begun to utter my usual words of reassurance [of neutrality], when I sensed something odd in the atmosphere, and stopping, reached instead for my revolver.

Faces turned to me in the lantern glow. But then almost immediately the gazes returned to the far corner where a dozen or so children had crowded around something down on the ground. Some of the children were poking with sticks at whatever it was. . . . It was though I had disturbed some dark ritual. . . . Perhaps it was because I heard a noise, or perhaps it was some sixth sense; but then I found myself, revolver still drawn, moving towards the circle of children. . . . I then saw in the dim red glow the figure of a Japanese soldier lying quite still on his side. . . . His face and hair were covered in dirt and speckled with blood. For all that, I recognized Akira with no difficulty. (pp. 265–66)

Akira, we know, is his best friend from childhood, the Japanese boy who lived next door and with whom he concocted elaborate detective games. Insisting that Akira is his long-lost friend, Christopher promises to help this wounded soldier.

We may recognize Christopher's promises and efforts as the actions of a desperate man who merely requires assistance in his own self-deluded pursuit, which misses the larger point: there is a war being waged here. His recognition of Akira, the novel makes clear, is a mistake. Nonetheless, after this has become evident to Christopher—he and "Akira" arrive to the house to find not his parents held hostage but a scene of death and destruction— he does not dismiss him; to the members of the Japanese army who find them and who arrest "Akira" as a traitor, he asks what became of him and whether he can see him again (p. 296). The novel opposes Christopher's concern for this man to the strident nationalist and imperialist rationale of a Japanese army general, who warns Christopher not to become "too sentimental" (p. 296). He defends the invasion of China and its resulting bloodshed on the basis of his nation's journey to greatness. As the general tells Christopher, "if Japan is to become a great nation, . . . it is necessary. Just as it once was for England" (p. 297). Rather than as a mistake, we can see Christopher's concern for "Akira" as a brave extension of his willingness to differently imagine his attachments. Disrupting what Homi Bhabha terms the naturalizability of the national (1994, p. 87), the novel represents Christopher as a mimic man who, despite his diligent efforts[3], "has never felt really at home" in England (Ishiguro, 2000, p. 274)[4]. He tells "Akira" as he tends to him that he considers the International Settlement his "home village" (p. 274). This section suggests that it is not a romantic but an ethical relation that the novel is truly interested in.

The responsibility that Christopher takes for this soldier is not an adequate reply or retort to the accelerations of militarism and fascism that the novel touches on; but, as I noted in Chapter Three, an emphasis on and attention to the particular claim and the contingent situation may sharpen a politics, initiating what Derek Attridge terms "a process of constant reappraisal and self-redefinition through which moral injunctions [and political generalizations] are tested, reaffirmed, or remade" (1994, p. 76). This process resonates with progressive thinking that remains skeptical of *final* visions of justice or of the just society, which is not to say uncommitted to making judgments or envisioning justice; feminists, for instance, know how such visions may be constructed at the expense of women[5]. If I began this study by taking a distance from Bruce Robbins's call to master a cosmopolitan ethics and politics, I want here to suggest that this reappraisal accords with his argument for an internationalism that is supple, contextual, and conjunctural, that mixes and maneuvers among different allegiances and aims[6].

As *When We Were Orphans* evidences in miniature, the fictions I have read in this study represent the (often unplanned for) realignment of affective and ethical identifications. They dramatize and negotiate the problems or difficulties that press on that realignment, like the scattered hegemonies that make antiretrovirals unavailable in Antigua or the various impediments to redistributive justice in South Africa. Without finding in ethics the solution or an alternative to politics, they contend instead with the necessary, and productive, negotiation between the singular demand or the individual response and collective action. Taken from Bhabha (1994, p. 18), the title of this Afterword expresses the forward-looking and future-oriented impulses of these works. While they do not imagine final victory, these cosmopolitan fictions envision doing justice as a struggle that must be engaged.

# Notes

## NOTES TO THE INTRODUCTION

1. See, for example, chapter eight of *Feeling Global* (Robbins, 1999). This work is addressed to those people "who have a personal, and perhaps also a professional, interest in the appalling record of global injustice," who, Robbins argues, must not feel compelled "to disavow or abstain from using whatever power they come to possess" (p. 5).

2. "Difficult as it may be to make a plural for cosmos, it is now assumed more and more that worlds, like nations, come in different sizes and styles," Bruce Robbins writes (1998, p. 2); *Cosmopolitics* (Cheah & Robbins, 1998) demonstrates just this point.

3. This is the distinction that Giles Gunn draws in his reading of Jay (2001, p. 22); Gunn provides a useful, and corrective, disciplinary history of globalizing literary studies, pointing out that the field of comparative literature "was from the beginning designed to take seriously the representational traffic across national and cultural as well as generic and, less frequently, historical borders" (p. 17).

4. Suggesting that he has "no country or society to speak for or write about" (Ishiguro & Kenzaburo, 1991, p. 115), Ishiguro also considers himself a homeless writer (p. 115); as *The Unconsoled* suggests, however, not knowing just where your home is is not the same as being homeless; it is, rather, to recognize the multiplicities of belonging or connection.

5. Informing my understanding of this process of worlding is Homi Bhabha's assertion that "the critic must attempt to fully realize, and take responsibility for, the unspoken, unrepresented pasts that haunt the historical present" (1994, p. 12).

6. As Bruce Robbins argues, "arriving at anything like a satisfactory politics in the face of present global conditions" is nothing short of difficult (2002, p. 94).

7. In a response to this suspicion, the editors of *The Turn to Ethics* claim that "rather than leading away from ethics, [the suspicion itself has] helped

reinvigorate the intellectual field" (Garber, Hanssen & Walkowitz, 2000, p. ix)—as I hope this study demonstrates.

8. *Feeling Global* identifies as "the goal for the political imagination for the next millennium" the search for ways that support for causes such as feminism, human rights, and the environment "could be channeled into struggles that recognize some, though not all, of what each party wants" (Robbins, 1999, p. 173).

9. Barbara Johnson suggests that literature "is not to be understood as a predetermined set of [cultural] works but as a mode of cultural work" (1998, p. 13), a suggestion that informs my distinction between text and work. In making this distinction, I am also indebted to Derek Attridge, who uses "work" to emphasize the written object's authoredness and inventiveness (see *The Singularity of Literature*, 2003, pp. 100–103 in particular).

10. I take these terms from Bruce Robbins (1999, p. 155), who reminds us not to associate capital only with the global; as he insists, we cannot treat capitalism "as if it came from somewhere else, as if Americans derived no benefit from it . . ." (p. 154).

11. See Tina Rosenberg's discussion of the Clinton administration's 1999 "conversion" (28 January 2001, p. 58); surprisingly, the Bush administration has not reversed the Clinton administration's decision not to seek sanctions against countries that invoke compulsory licensing.

## NOTES TO CHAPTER ONE

1. Ishiguro won the Booker Prize for *The Remains of the Day* in 1989; his thickly textured portrait, painted by Peter Edwards, hangs in the National Portrait Gallery in London.

2. See reviews of the novel by Wyndham (23 October 1995), Wood (21 December 1995), and Menand (19 October 1995), respectively.

3. Jay McInerney's review declares that Stevens wins the comparison—next to the autistic adolescent in Haddon's *The Curious Incident of the Dog in the Night-Time*, McInerney asserts, Stevens looks like Zorba the Greek (16 June 2003, p. 5)—but it is still a notable one.

4. I echo Derek Attridge's expression "an everyday impossibility" here (see chapter ten of *The Singularity of Literature*, 2004). For him, impossible does not mean uncommon but exceptional—and exceptional in the sense of not fitting comfortably into our established codes and frameworks. I am making a related distinction between ethics as the experience of the not-possible and ethics as actually not-possible (see next sentence and endnote below). This distinction is sharpened by Derrida's strident analysis of the social organization of the possible. As he argues, "civilized" society, in its institution of the laws of the market and the mechanisms of external debt, "*puts to* death or . . . *allows* to die of hunger and disease tens

of millions of children (those neighbors or fellow humans that ethics or the discourse of the rights of man refer to) . . ." (1995, p. 86).

5.  I owe this distinction to Gayatri Chakravorty Spivak (1995, p. xxv).

6.  Such a disjunction is also that between justice and the law; as Cornell reminds us, "[w]e are called to work within the law but we should not conflate law with justice" (1991, p. 116). My next chapter takes up the just remaking of the law.

7.  Here we might also look to Bruce Robbins's assertion that the novel, intensifying the conflicting demands on Ryder, also gestures beyond them to a possible abundance of commitment (2001b, p. 437). Ishiguro's play with time and space, he argues, "messes with the zero-sum game of everyday common sense" (p. 437), which pits the family against work, the domestic against the international. Cornell's understanding of responsibility as infinite and yet concrete—and hence subject to negotiation and rethinking—invites a challenge to this everyday common sense as well. In writing and revising this chapter, I am indebted to Robbins's revaluations of Ishiguro's characters' "misplaced" senses of duty and to his observation of his works' darkly funny, and surprisingly utopian, elements (see Robbins, 2001a and 2001b).

8.  Iyer makes a similar observation at the end of his review, without pursuing its implications; as he observes of the novel, "sometimes the effects are so calculated and careful (in the book as well as in the characters) that I felt as if I were hearing about sadness rather than feeling it . . ." (28 April 1995, p. 22).

9.  These claims are sharpened by David Rieff's rejection of the term humanitarian intervention altogether; he prefers war (see Rieff, 26 June 2003).

10. To be clear, I am countering this term to the dominant discourse of globalization, which Jay's own insistence on the multidirectionality and historical specificity of cultural flows complicates (see Paul Jay, 2001).

## NOTES TO CHAPTER TWO

1.  In her reading of Kincaid's *Lucy,* Spivak asserts that the novel challenges "the self-indulgences of contemporary diasporism" (2001, p. 345); for one thing, it does not allow the simple attributions of guilt and responsibility—we are here because you are guilty" (p. 344)—that we might expect. Like *Lucy,* Ondaatje's novel allows Anil a more complex stance toward her own migration (made under circumstances far different from Lucy's), some of which is revealed in the haunting of her identity that I note at the end of this chapter. The novel does not grant us a vision of either full return or easy departure.

2.  As Ondaatje's earlier work, which takes us into an East Louisiana state hospital (see next paragraph), suggests, these standards may be useful against

the very powers with which they are bound up (see Robbins, 1999, p. 74; see also Hurrell, 1999, p. 278).

3. This statistic is cited by Ondaatje in *Coming Through Slaughter* (1976, p. 144).

4. For this analysis, see *Slaughter Among Neighbors: The Political Origins of Communal Violence* (Human Rights Watch, 1995).

5. I take these terms from Bruce Robbins, who argues that one may also draw energy and authority from the very refusal of virtue (1999, p. 119).

6. As J. Swenson (his translator) points out, for Balibar, citizenship "[designates] rights and, in particular, a 'right to politics'" (see Balibar, 1998, p. 228, note 10). Nationality, "the status of belonging, generally in an exclusive fashion, to a particular nation, by birth or naturalization" is more passive (p. 228).

7. We might extend this point to note that the border, in Balibar's analysis, is no longer a limit but "a thing within the space of the political itself" (1998, p. 220); it is itself a newly contested space.

8. This refusal sharpens its detection from "social criticism" (Lehman, 2000, p. 110) to social critique, not only illuminating the social order but also rejecting its norms, like state-sponsored terrorism.

9. This dynamic is at work in *In the Skin of a Lion* and *The English Patient;* in the former, Patrick's insistence that "[t]his is only a love story" (Ondaatje, 1997, p. 160), is belied by the narrative itself, which sets its romance within the framework of labor organization and political resistance.

## NOTES TO CHAPTER THREE

1. While her mother can imagine bright professional futures for her baby sons, she cannot do so for Lucy herself.

2. As Sarah Brophy argues, *My Brother* suggests that Kincaid has crossed the line into the North "at her own expense" (2002, p. 269), losing her ties to her family and to Antigua; Kincaid, she argues, "is the Drew family's missing person" (p. 270). Her welcome separation from her mother, and her attempts to remove herself from her family, suggests that this loss is an ambivalent one.

3. Brophy points out the disturbing link between his disease and his blackness (2002, p. 272), repeated elsewhere in the work.

4. Referencing one of these moments—"in his life there had been no flowering, his life was the opposite of that, a flowering, his life was like the bud that sets but, instead of opening into a flower, turns brown and falls off at your feet" (1997, pp. 162–63)—Brophy suggests that his is not a life "to reconstruct as would ordinarily be conceived of in the conventions of Western biography or autobiography" (2002, p. 274).

5. I owe this idea to Gayatri Chakravorty Spivak, who seeks in her reading of *Lucy* not to "write off black specificity by claiming history-transcending

universality for great art" but "to question why white specificity [is] unmarked as white" (2001, p. 352); she finds in *Lucy* "a longing for unmarked humanity, without denying black specificity" (p. 352).

6. Even more pointedly, she explains that does not want to be rejoined with him at some later date: ". . . when the minister preached a sermon about us [her brothers and her mother] all being reunited at some later date, I did not like that at all, I wanted to tell him that I did not want to see these people with whom I had shared so much . . .—I did not want to be with any of these people again in another world" (Kincaid, 1997, pp. 193–94).

7. Issued in 1998 by the UN High Commissioner for Human Rights and the UNAIDS Secretariat, the International Guidelines on HIV/AIDS assert that there is no public health rationale for state restrictions on the movement or residence of people based on HIV status. For this information, see the UNAIDS *(Barcelona) Report on the Global HIV/AIDS Epidemic* (2002).

8. I take my terms from Kruger as well; as he argues, "the narrative of inexorable individual disease encourages the view of people with AIDS as passive victims, helpless in the face of an implacable enemy," a narrative that "present[s] the picture of a 'battle' already lost: individuals and populations affected with AIDS are irretrievable" (1996, pp. 79–80).

9. As the authors of 'Cosmopolitanisms' note, ". . . all feminisms have had to struggle with their own universalisms" (Pollock, Bhabha, Breckenridge & Chakrabarty, 2000, p. 583), a struggle from which they suggest cosmopolitanism itself can learn.

10. Robbins uses the term "ethical ennui" to describe the nationalist project in his critique of the critics of Martha Nussbaum's cosmopolitanism, who refuse to grapple with her numbers, "the relative and absolute indicators of one population's wealth and another's desperate, almost unfathomable misery" (1999, p. 154). "Who among her respondents talks about transfers of wealth? Who offers to explain why such ideas are aborted in the richer nations, before they can even be proposed, victims of an ethical ennui or paralysis that is, perhaps, the truest face of nationalism in the so-called developed world?" (p. 155).

11. As Brophy notes, she sees in him "a wasted potential for heterosexual and economic productivity" (2002, p. 269); Kincaid notes again later that Devon dies "with none of the traditional attachments ordinary to a man his age—thirty-three—a companion of some kind, children, his own house, even a house he rented, his own bed . . ." (1997, p. 173). This critique is differently coded at other moments, when she finds in him a difficult struggle to separate himself from their mother (p. 78; see also p. 53).

12. Robbins argues no in his reading of *Lucy*, to which this final section is indebted—see "Upward mobility in the postcolonial era" in *Feeling Global: Internationalism in Distress* (Robbins, 1999).

13. In an argument I cite at various moments in this study, Bhabha suggests that it is our task to reveal the "domestic" "as an uncanny site/sign of the

native, the indigenous, as a kind of 'vernacular' cosmopolitanism . . ."
(1996, p. 202). "Bear in mind . . ." he writes, "that the 'vernacular' shares an
etymological root with the 'domestic' but adds to it—like the 'un' that turns
*heimlich* into *unheimlich* . . ." (p. 202).

## NOTES TO CHAPTER FOUR

1.  I adapt these words from Gayatri Chakravorty Spivak who, in a point I will
    return to at the end of the chapter, urges us in a different direction from
    goodwill; she sets as our task the struggle "to learn to be responsible as we
    study to be political" (1998, p. 337).
2.  Derek Attridge makes this point, asserting of Coetzee's work that "there can
    be no question about the ceaseless, intense engagement with [South Africa]
    and, more specifically, with its political and social history . . ." (2000,
    p. 99); I owe the reference to this interview to his "Grace."
3.  On Coetzee's internationalism, see also Attridge (1992, p. 230) and Head
    (1997, p. 18).
4.  The reference is to Helen Small's MLA talk (29 December 2001), in which
    she read *Disgrace* as a novel of mid-life crisis, arguing that David Lurie's
    claim that he was too old to change was "spurious," a way of opting out of
    history. I have much less sympathy for Lurie than I do for Mrs. Curren, but
    see in these novels—on the level of character and narrative—an impulse
    toward, rather than an opting out of, history.
5.  For Attridge, the interactions with John provoke Mrs. Curren to "a new
    understanding of the political necessity and inevitability of [his] activism
    and activities, and therefore of a conflict—the conflict between the ethical
    and the political, which is also a conflict *within* both the ethical and the
    political . . ." (1994, p. 75). My reading aims to historicize the ethical
    responsibility she recognizes, without losing sight of the conflict between
    and within the singular and the general. Homi Bhabha's analysis of the pas-
    sage from the material to the metaphoric returns me to it.
6.  I refer to Mrs. Curren's acknowledgment of the ways in which landscape
    may be mystified; looking with Vercueil at an account of an English-
    woman traveling through Palestine and Syria, she observes that "[b]y
    some trick of perspective the illustrator had given to moonlit encamp-
    ments, desert crags, ruined temples an air of looming mystery. No one
    had done that for South Africa: made it into a land of mystery" (Coetzee,
    1998, p. 83). It has, however, been made into a place of emptiness and
    absence.
7.  For this argument, see Cornell, 1995, pp. 84–85.
8.  I take this point from Attridge, 2000, p. 105.
9.  O'Brien (2001) actually misuses Gayatri Chakravorty Spivak to help make
    this point; in the instance he cites from—Spivak's conclusion that there are

no victories that aren't also warnings—she is addressing the victories or successes of justice, not those of violence.

10. Attridge asserts that the novel's critique "is aimed not at a local issue but at a global phenomenon of the end of the twentieth century; those who work in educational systems in many parts of the world can tell their own stories of the 'great rationalization,' and of course the syndrome goes well beyond the walls of the academy" (2000, p. 101).

11. It is Bill Readings's analysis of the university "in ruins" that I am drawing on in this paragraph (1996, see pp. 10–12 especially).

12. The novel's implicit critique isn't the one that David is making; his comments may be differently angled toward the bottom line, suggesting that one of the costs of South African reconstruction is the systematization or schematization of life (see Attridge, 2001, p. 118).

13. There is no direct parallel with the TRC here, as it specifically did *not* require its testifiers to repent or express remorse. However, Antje Krog notes the confusion over its secular status that stemmed from its use of the terminology of confession and forgiveness; she quotes General Tienie Groenewald, "I confess to God, not to Tutu" (1998, p. 17).

14. I take this point from Elleke Boehmer, who asks the question I am attempting to answer in this discussion: "Do silent women-in-pain remain the ground on which a new society is brought into being?" (2003, p. 5).

## NOTES TO THE AFTERWORD

1. That work is itself meaningful is a point that Bruce Robbins makes in his readings of Ishiguro's novels and their interests in professionalism; see "The village of the liberal managerial class" (2001a) and "Very busy just now: globalization and harriedness" (2001b).

2. Finding in *The Remains of the Day* "the germ of the dreamscape that entirely takes over in *The Unconsoled*" (8 June 1995, p. 30), Amit Chaudhuri hints at Darlington Hall's own Gothicism, seeing it less as "an old British building, with its resonances of personal memory and history, than a Kafkaesque castle, a place to get lost in" (p. 30).

3. Warned that spending time in Shanghai will turn him "into a Chinaman" (Ishiguro, 2000, p. 20), Christopher as a child asks his "uncle" Philip to help him become more English by allowing him to copy him.

4. Like Christopher, Ishiguro does imagines himself "a very English Englishman"—or, in his case, "a very Japanese Japanese" either (Ishiguro & Kenzaburo, p. 115).

5. Diane Elam makes this point (1994, pp. 105–6), which, I have suggested, motivates a commitment to the non-finality of justice.

6. See the introduction and first chapter of *Feeling Global: Internationalism in Distress* (Robbins, 1999).

# Bibliography

Adelman, Gary. (2001) "Doubles on the rocks: Kazuo Ishiguro's *The Unconsoled.*" *Critique: Studies in Contemporary Fiction,* 42(2): 166–179.

Amnesty International. (3 June 1998) "Questions and answers concerning the proposed permanent International Criminal Court (ICC)." Online. Available: <http://web.amnesty.org/library/index/ENGIOR400171998> (accessed 6 January 2005).

Anderson, Perry. (1997) "The Europe to Come," in Peter Gowan & Perry Anderson (eds) *The Question of Europe,* London: Verso, 126–145.

Associated Press. (7 July 2002) "Caribbeans to buy AIDS drugs at discounts." *New York Times,* late edition: A4.

Attridge, Derek. (1992) "Oppressive silence: J. M. Coetzee's *Foe* and the politics of the canon," in Karen R. Lawrence (ed.) *Decolonizing Tradition: New Views of Twentieth-Century "British" Literary Canons.* Urbana: University of Illinois Press, 212–238.

———. (1994) "Trusting the other: Ethics and politics in J. M. Coetzee's *Age of Iron.*" *The South Atlantic Quarterly,* 93(1): 59–82.

———. (2000) "Age of bronze, state of grace: Music and dogs in Coetzee's *Disgrace.*" *Novel,* 34(1): 98–121.

———. (2004) *The Singularity of Literature.* London and New York: Routledge.

Attwell, David. (1998) "'Dialogue'" and 'fulfillment' in J. M. Coetzee's *Age of Iron,*" in Derek Attridge & Rosemary Jolly (eds) *Writing South Africa: Literature, Apartheid, and Democracy, 1970–1996.* Cambridge: Cambridge University Press. 166–179.

Balibar, Étienne. (1998) "The borders of Europe," in Pheng Cheah & Bruce Robbins (eds) *Cosmopolitics: Thinking and Feeling Beyond the Nation.* Minneapolis: University of Minnesota Press, 216–229.

Barkan, Elazar. (2000) *The Guilt of Nations: Restitution and Negotiating Historical Injustices.* New York: W.W. Norton & Co.

Barnard, Rita. (1994) "Dream topographies: J. M. Coetzee and the South African pastoral." *The South Atlantic Quarterly,* 93(1): 33–57.

BBC News. (23 November 2000) "South Africa's child sex trafficking nightmare." Online. Available: <http://news.bbc.co.uk/1/hi/world/africa/1037215.stm> (accessed 31 January 2005).

Becker, Elizabeth. (26 August 2002) "U.S. issues warning to Europeans in dispute over New Court." *New York Times,* late edition: A10.

Bhabha, Homi K. (1994) *The Location of Culture.* London: Routledge.

——. (1996) "Unsatisfied: notes on vernacular cosmopolitanism," in Peter C. Pfeiffer & Laura Garcia-Moreno (eds) *Text and Narration.* Columbia, S.C.: Camden House, 191–207.

Blair, Tony. (23 April 1999) "Interview with Jim Lehrer." *PBS: NewsHour.* Online. Available: <http://www.pbs.org/newshour/bb/europe/jan-june99/blair_4–23.html> (accessed 31 January 2005).

Boehmer, Elleke. (2003) "Not saying sorry, not speaking pain: Gender implications in *Disgrace,*" in Bruce Bennett, Susan Cowan, Jacqueline Lo, Satendra Nandan & Jen Webb. (eds) *Resistance and Reconciliation: Writing in the Commonwealth.* Canberra: Association for Commonwealth Literature and Language Studies, 29–46.

Brophy, Sarah. (2002) "Angels in Antigua: The diasporic of melancholy in Jamaica Kincaid's *My Brother.*" *PMLA,* 117(2): 265–277.

Buell, Lawrence. (1999) "Introduction: In pursuit of ethics." *PMLA* 114(1): 7–19.

Butler, Judith. (1996) "Universality in culture," in Martha C. Nussbaum & Joshua Cohen (eds) *For Love of Country: Debating the Limits of Patriotism.* Boston: Beacon Press, 45–52.

Caruth, Cathy. (1992) *Unclaimed Experience: Trauma, Narrative, and History.* Baltimore: Johns Hopkins University Press.

Castle, Terry. (1995) *The Female Thermometer: Eighteenth-Century Culture and the Invention of the Uncanny.* New York: Oxford University Press.

Chaudhuri, Amit. (8 June 1995) "Unlike Kafka." *London Review of Books,* 30–31.

Cheah, Pheng & Robbins, Bruce (eds) (1998) *Cosmopolitics: Thinking and Feeling Beyond the Nation.* Minneapolis: University of Minnesota Press.

Coetzee, J. M. (1988) *White Writing: On the Culture of Letters in South Africa.* New Haven, CT: Yale University Press.

——. (1998) *Age of Iron.* New York: Penguin. (Orig. pub. 1990).

——. (1999) *Disgrace.* New York: Viking.

——. (2001) "What is a classic? A lecture." *Stranger Shores: Literary Essays, 1986–99.* New York: Viking, 1–17.

Cornell, Drucilla. (1991) *Beyond Accommodation: Ethical Feminism, Deconstruction, and the Law.* New York: Routledge.

——. (1995) "What is ethical feminism?" in Seyla Benhabib, Judith Butler, Drucilla Cornell & Nancy Fraser (eds) *Feminist Contentions: A Philosophical Exchange.* New York: Routledge, 75–106.

Critchley, Simon & Kearney, Richard. (2001) "Preface," in Jacques Derrida, *On Cosmopolitanism and Forgiveness.* London: Routledge, vii–xii.

Crossette, Barbara. (4 April 2002) "Washington is criticized for growing reluctance to sign treaties." *New York Times,* late edition: A5.

Derrida, Jacques. (1995) *The Gift of Death.* Chicago: University of Chicago Press.

——. (1996) "Adieu." *Critical Inquiry,* 23: 1–10.

——. (2001) *On Cosmopolitanism and Forgiveness.* London: Routledge. (Orig. pub. 1997).

Durrant, Samuel. (1999) "Bearing witness to apartheid. J. M. Coetzee's inconsolable works of mourning." *Contemporary Literature,* 3: 430–463.

Eder, Richard. (2 June 1999) "Old bliss, in a new arrondissement." *New York Times,* late edition, E8.

Elam, Diane. (1994) *Feminism and Deconstruction: Ms. en Abyme.* London: Routledge.

Falk, Richard. (2000) *Human Rights Horizons: The Pursuit of Justice in a Globalizing World.* New York: Routledge.

Freud, Sigmund. (1958) *The Interpretation of Dreams.* New York: Basic Books.

Garber, Marjorie, Hanssen, Beatrice & Walkowitz, Rebecca (eds) (2000) *The Turn to Ethics.* New York: Routledge.

Gibson, Andrew. (1999) *Postmodernity, Ethics, and the Novel: From Leavis to Levinas.* London: Routledge.

Grewal, Inderpal & Kaplan, Caren (eds) (1994) *Scattered Hegemonies: Postmodernity and Transnational Feminist Practice.* Minneapolis: University of Minnesota Press.

Gunn, Giles. (2001) "Introduction: Globalizing literary studies." *PMLA,* 116(1): 16–31.

Hall, Stuart. (1996) "The problem of ideology: Marxism without guarantees," in David Morely & Kuan-Hsing Chen (eds) *Stuart Hall: Critical Dialogues in Cultural Studies.* London: Routledge, 25–46.

Head, Dominic. (1997) *J. M. Coetzee.* Cambridge: Cambridge University Press.

Heble, Ajay. (1994) "'Rumours of topography': The cultural politics of Michael Ondaatje's *Running in the Family.*" *Essays on Canadian Writing,* 53: 186–203.

Honig, Bonnie. (2001) *Democracy and the Foreigner.* Princeton: Princeton University Press.

Human Rights Watch. (n.d.) "International justice." Online. Available: <http://hrw.org/justice/about.htm> (accessed 6 January 2005).

——. (1995) *Slaughter Among Neighbors: The Political Origins of Communal Violence.* New Haven, CT: Yale University Press.

——. (2002) "World Report 2002: Sri Lanka." Online. Available: <http://www.hrw.org/wr2k2/asia10.html#top> (accessed 6 January 2005).

Hurrell, Andrew. (1999) "Power, principles and prudence: Protecting human rights in a deeply divided world," in Tim Dunne & Nicholas J. Wheeler (eds) *Human Rights in Global Politics,* 177–202.

Ishiguro, Kazuo. (1993) *The Remains of the Day.* New York: Vintage International. (Orig. pub. 1989).

——. (1995) *The Unconsoled.* New York: Knopf.

——. (2000) *When We Were Orphans.* New York: Knopf.

Ishiguro, Kazuo & Kenzaburo, Oe. (1991) "The novelist in today's world: A conversation." *Boundary 2: An International Journal of Literature and Culture,* 18(3): 109–122.

Iyer, Pico. (28 April 1995) "The butler didn't do it, again." *Times Literary Supplement,* 22.

Jameson, Fredric. (1999) "History lessons," in Neil Leach (ed.) *Architecture and Revolution: Contemporary Perspectives on Central and Eastern Europe.* London: Routledge, 69–80.

Jay, Paul. (2001) "Beyond discipline? Globalization and the future of English." *PMLA,* 116(1): 32–47.

——. (29 December 2001) "Is global fiction postcolonial?" Paper presented at the MLA Convention, New Orleans, LA.

Johnson, Barbara. (1998) *The Feminist Difference: Literature, Psychoanalysis, Race, and Gender.* Cambridge: Harvard University Press.

Kaplan, Caren. (1994) "The politics of location as transnational feminist practice," in Inderpal Grewal & Caren Kaplan (eds) *Scattered Hegemonies: Postmodernity and Transnational Female Practices.* Minneapolis: University of Minnesota Press, 137–152.

Keenan, Thomas. (2002) "Publicity and indifference (Sarajevo on television)." *PMLA* (117)1: 104–116.

Kincaid, Jamaica. (1983) *At the Bottom of a River.* New York: Farrar, Straus & Giroux.

——. (1985) *Annie John.* New York: Farrar, Straus & Giroux.

——. (1991) *Lucy.* New York: Plume. (Orig. pub. 1990).

——. (1997) *My Brother.* New York: Farrar, Straus & Giroux.

——. (2001) *Talk Stories.* New York: Farrar, Straus & Giroux.

Krog, Antje. (1998) *Country of My Skull.* London: Jonathan Cape.

Kruger, Steven F. (1996) *AIDS Narratives: Gender and Sexuality, Fiction and Science.* New York: Garland Publishing.

LeClair, Tom. (19 June 2000) "Sri Lanka's patients." *The Nation,* 31–33.

Lehman, David. (2000) *The Perfect Murder: A Study in Detection.* Ann Arbor: University of Michigan Press. (Orig. pub. 1989).

Lewis, Barry. (2000) *Kazuo Ishiguro.* New York: St. Martin's Press.

Lewis, Neil A. (5 May 2002) "U.S. set to renounce its role in pact for world tribunal." *New York Times,* late edition: A18.

Mamdani, Mahmood. (26 June 2003) "Humanitarian intervention: A forum." *The Nation.* Online. Available: <http://www.thenation.com/doc.mhtml?i=200307 14&c=5&s=forum> (accessed 1 February 2005).

——. (2000) "The truth according to the TRC," in Ifi Amadiume & Abdullahi Ahmed An-Na'im (eds) *The Politics of Memory: Truth, Healing, and Social Justice.* London: Zed Books, 176–183.

Marais, Michael. (2000) "'Little enough, less than little, nothing': Ethics, engagement and change in the fiction of J. M. Coetzee." *Modern Fiction Studies,* 46(1): 159–182.

McClure, John. (n.d.) *Postmodern/Postsecular: The Work of Religion in Contemporary Fiction.* Unpublished manuscript.

McInerney, Jay. (16 June 2003) "The remains of the dog." *The New York Times Book Review,* 5.

Menand, Louis. (15 October 1995) "Anxious in dreamland." *The New York Times Book Review,* 7.

Midgley, Mary. "Toward an ethic of global responsibility," in Tim Dunne & Nicholas J. Wheeler (eds) (1999) *Human Rights in Global Politics.* Cambridge: Cambridge University Press, 160–174.

Morphet, Tony. (1987) "Two interviews with J.M Coetzee, 1983 and 1987." *Tri-Quarterly* 69: 454–464.

Mulvey, Laura. (1999) "Reflections on disgraced monuments," in Neil Leach (ed.) *Architecture and Revolution: Contemporary Perspectives on Central and Eastern Europe.* London: Routledge, 219–227.

O'Brien, Anthony. (2001) *Against Normalization: Writing Radical Democracy in South Africa.* Durham, NC: Duke University Press.

Ondaatje, Michael. (1976) *Coming Through Slaughter.* New York: Norton.

——. (1993a) *Running in the Family.* New York: Vintage International. (Orig. pub. 1982).

——. (1993b) *The English Patient.* New York: Vintage International. (Orig. pub. 1992).

——. (1997) *In the Skin of a Lion.* New York: Vintage International. (Orig. pub. 1987).

——. (2000) *Anil's Ghost.* New York: Knopf.

Pollock, Sheldon, Bhabha, Homi K., Breckenridge, Carol A. & Chakrabarty, Dipesh. (2000) "Cosmopolitanisms." *Public Culture,* 12(3): 577–589.

Porter, Dennis. (1981) *The Pursuit of Crime: Art and Ideology in Detective Fiction.* New Haven, CT: Yale University Press.

Pyrhönen, Heta. (1999) *Mayhem and Murder: Narrative and Moral Problems in the Detective Story.* Toronto: University of Toronto Press.

Rand, Nicholas & Torok, Maria. (1997) *Questions for Freud: The Secret History of Psychoanalysis.* Cambridge, MA: Harvard University Press.

Readings, Bill. (1996) *The University in Ruins.* Cambridge, MA: Harvard University Press.

Rieff, David. (1995) *Slaughterhouse: Bosnia and the Failure of the West.* New York: Simon & Schuster.

——. (26 June 2003) "Humanitarian intervention: A forum." *The Nation.* Online. Available: <http://www.thenation.com/doc.mhtml?i=20030714&c= 6&s= forum> (accessed 29 January 2005).

Robbins, Bruce. (1998) "Introduction part one: Actually existing cosmopolitanism," in Pheng Cheah & Bruce Robbins (eds) *Cosmopolitics: Thinking and Feeling Beyond the Nation.* Minneapolis: University of Minnesota Press, 1–19.

Robbins, Bruce. (1999) *Feeling Global: Internationalism in Distress*. New York: New York University Press.

——. (2001a) "The village of the liberal managerial class," in Vinay Dharwadker (ed.) *Cosmopolitan Geographies*. New York: Routledge, 15–32.

——. (2001b) "Very busy just now: Globalization and harriedness in Ishiguro's *The Unconsoled*." *Comparative Literature* 53(4): 426–441.

——. (2002) "The sweatshop sublime." *PMLA,* 117(1): 84–97.

Rorty, Richard. (October 10 1995) "Consolation prize." *Village Voice Literary Supplement,* 40(41), p. 13.

Rosenberg, Tina. (28 January 2001) "How to solve the world's AIDS crisis: Look at Brazil." *New York Times Magazine,* 26–31, 52, 58–63.

Roth, Marty. (1995) *Foul and Fair Play: Reading Genre in Classic Detective Fiction*. Athens, GA: University of Georgia Press.

Simmons, Diane. (1994) *Jamaica Kincaid*. New York: Maxwell MacMillan International.

Small, Helen. (29 December 2001) "Periodizing the present." Paper presented at the MLA Convention, New Orleans, LA.

Spivak, Gayatri Chakravorty. (1985) "Three women's texts and a critique of imperialism," in Henry Louis Gates Jr. (ed.) *"Race," Writing, and Difference*. Chicago: University of Chicago Press, 262–280.

——. (1991) "Theory in the margin: Coetzee's *Foe* reading Defoe's *Crusoe/Roxanna*," in Jonathan Arac & Barbara Johnson (eds) *Consequences of Theory*. Baltimore: Johns Hopkins University Press, 154–180.

——. (1993) "Woman in difference." *Outside in the Teaching Machine*. New York: Routledge, 77–95.

——. (1995) "Translator's preface and afterword," in Mahasweta Devi, *Imaginary Maps: Three Stories*. New York: Routledge, xxiii–ix and 197–205.

——. (1998) "Cultural talks in the hot peace: Revisiting the 'global village,'" in Pheng Cheah & Bruce Robbins (eds) *Cosmopolitics: Thinking and Feeling Beyond the Nation*. Minneapolis: University of Minnesota Press, 329–348.

——. (2001) "Thinking cultural questions in 'pure' literary terms," in Paul Gilroy, Lawrence Grossberg & Angela McRobbie (eds) *Without Guarantees: In Honour of Stuart Hall*. London: Verso, 335–357.

Steiner, George. (1996) *No Passion Spent*. New Haven, CT: Yale University Press.

Strouse, Jean. (7 July 2002) "Capitalism depends on character (editorial)." *New York Times,* late edition: A9.

Suleri, Sara. (1987). *Meatless Days*. Chicago: University of Chicago Press.

Thomas, Ronald R. (1999) *Detective Fiction and the Rise of Forensic Science*. Cambridge: Cambridge University Press.

Truth and Reconciliation Commission. (1998) *Truth and Reconciliation Commission of South Africa Report*. (5 volumes). Cape Town: Truth and Reconciliation Commission.

UNAIDS. (2002) *Report on the Global HIV/AIDS Epidemic.* Online. Available: <http://www.unaids.org/html/pub/global-reports/barcelona/brglobal_aids_report_en_pdf.htm> (accessed 1 February 2005).

Updike, John. (15 May 2000) "Dangerous into beautiful: An expatriate novelist returns home." *The New Yorker,* 91–92.

Wood, Michael. (21 December 1995). "Sleepless Nights." *New York Review of Books,* 17–18.

Wyndham, Francis. (23 October 1995) "Nightmare Hotel." *The New Yorker,* 91–94.

Young, Hugo. (1999) *This Blessed Plot.* Woodstock, NY: The Overlook Press.

# Index